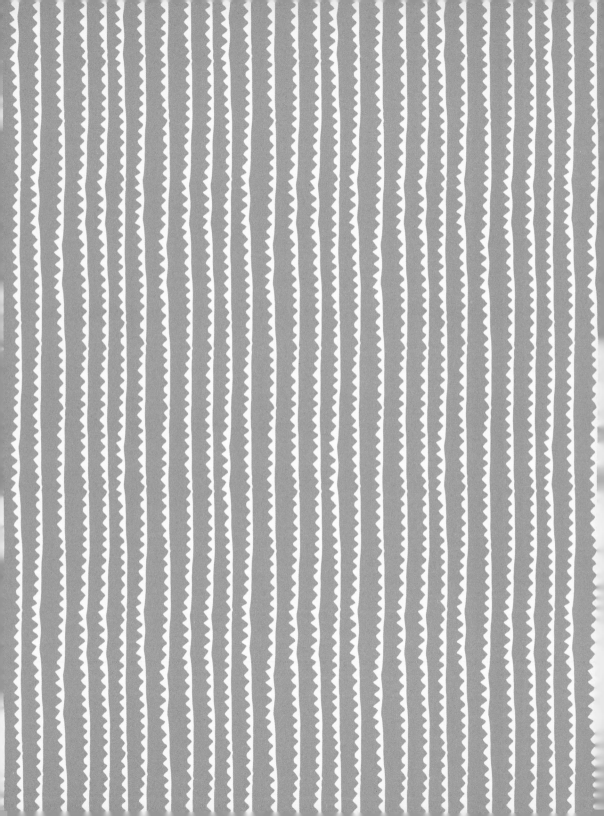

# Parks and Recreation

# Galentine's Day

## The Official Guide to Friendship, Fun, and Cocktails

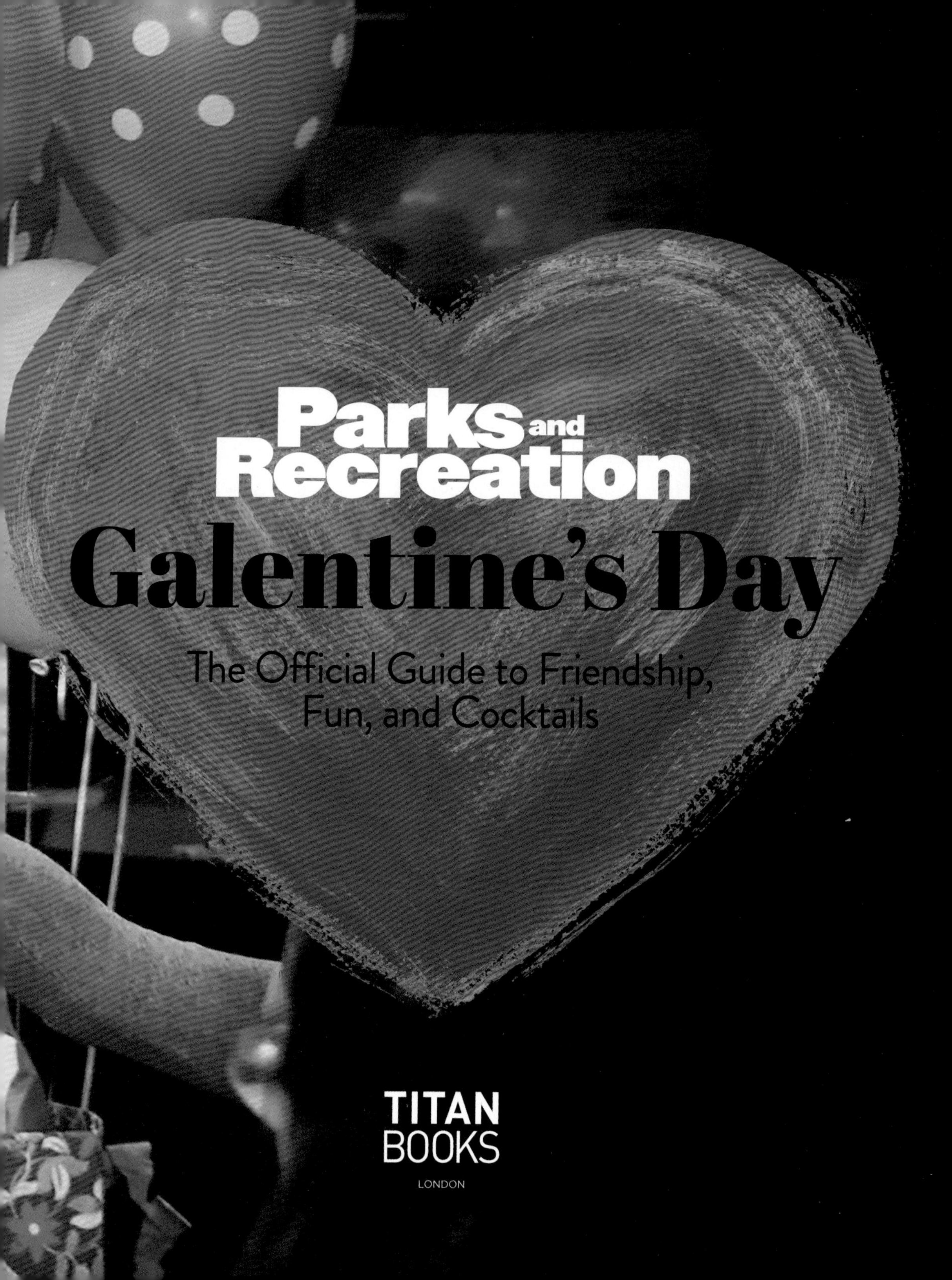

# Parks and Recreation

# Galentine's Day

## The Official Guide to Friendship, Fun, and Cocktails

**TITAN BOOKS**

LONDON

# Contents

**"What's Galentine's Day?** *Oh, it's only the best day of the year. Every February 13, my lady friends and I leave our husbands and our boyfriends at home, and we just come and kick it, breakfast style. Ladies celebrating ladies. It's like Lilith Fair, minus the angst. Plus frittatas."* — Leslie Knope

*"February 14, Valentine's Day, is about romance. But February 13, Galentine's Day, is about celebrating lady friends. It's wonderful, and it should be a national holiday."* — Leslie Knope

Ever since Leslie Knope celebrated that first Galentine's Day with waffles, frittatas, mimosas, hand-crocheted flower pens, mosaic portraits made from "the crushed bottles of your favorite diet soda," and a personalized 5,000-word essay on why each person present was so awesome, women around the world have been doing the same.

*Parks and Recreation Galentine's Day The Official Guide to Friendship, Fun, and Cocktails* is a gift to gal pals everywhere—a handbook for throwing a Galentine's Day soirée that will show your female clan just how you feel about each and every one of them.

While Leslie's petition to Congress to make Galentine's Day a national holiday was ignored, you're sure to have a successful celebration throwing any one of the themed parties laid out in the pages of this book—from a "Kickin' It Ladies' Style Brunch" (of course!), where everyone can just kick back and eat whipped-cream-topped waffles, to a "Sweet Crafternooner" that keeps guests busy making Hand-Crocheted Flower Pens and Galentine's Snow Globes while staying fortified with a selection of homemade sweets.

In keeping with Leslie's comprehensive approach to everything, each party is presented as a complete event with crafts projects, decorating ideas, and recipes. Think of it as a binder in the form of a book that will help you, as Leslie might say, "forge [your] own unique traditions in the fiery cauldron of friendship."

*"To girlfriends!"* — Leslie Knope

# Kickin' It Ladies' Style Brunch

Celebrate the most important ladies in your life this Galentine's Day the original way: with a spread of delicious breakfast foods (including frittatas and waffles, of course!), fabulous gifts and decorations, and creative party activities—all made by hand, Leslie Knope style, with love.

# No-Food-Finer-Than JJ's-Diner Waffles

*"We need to remember what's important in life: friends, waffles, and work. Or waffles, friends, work. Doesn't matter, but work is third."* — Leslie Knope

If you're like Leslie, you probably believe with all of your heart that your local diner has the best waffles in the world. But give these light and airy waffles a try and enjoy them with friends—and extra whipped cream, of course.

**SERVES 4 TO 6**

**PREP TIME:** 10 MINUTES

**COOK TIME:** 5 MINUTES PER WAFFLE

**WHAT YOU NEED**

2 cups all-purpose flour

1 teaspoon kosher salt

4 teaspoons baking powder

2 tablespoons sugar

2 large eggs

1½ cups whole milk, warmed

⅓ cup butter, melted

1 teaspoon pure vanilla extract

Toppings: Whipped cream, syrups of choice, assorted jams, and fresh fruit

**HOW YOU MAKE IT**

In a bowl, whisk together flour, salt, baking powder, and sugar. Preheat a waffle iron to 375°F.

In another bowl, beat eggs. Stir in milk, butter, and vanilla extract. Pour the milk mixture into the flour mixture; whisk gently just until blended (a few lumps are OK).

Ladle batter into the preheated waffle iron. Cook until golden and crisp, about 5 to 6 minutes. Repeat with remaining batter. Serve immediately with toppings.

**MAKE IT GLUTEN-FREE:** Use a gluten-free flour blend in place of the all-purpose flour.

**MAKE IT VEGAN:** Use equivalent amount of a plant-based egg product in place of the eggs. Substitute plant-based butter and milk for dairy butter and milk.

**ALLERGENS:** Wheat, dairy

EASY   GLUTEN-FREE

# Angst-Free Mini Frittatas

In an attempt to impress her new jet-setting beau, Justin, Leslie decides to throw a dinner party—and winds up demonstrating that she really has no idea how to throw a dinner party. You'll suffer no such fate with these cheesy, veggie-packed mini frittatas. They're full of flavor and so easy to make, the prospect of entertaining will fill you with delight, not dread.

**SERVES 6 TO 8**
**PREP TIME**: 10 MINUTES
**COOK TIME**: 20 MINUTES

**WHAT YOU NEED**
Cooking spray
8 large eggs
¼ cup milk
1 teaspoon Italian seasoning
¼ teaspoon kosher salt
¼ teaspoon freshly ground black pepper
1 cup finely diced ham (optional)
4 green onions, finely chopped
1 small zucchini, shredded and squeezed dry
½ small red pepper, finely chopped
1 cup shredded cheddar cheese

**HOW YOU MAKE IT**

Preheat oven to 350°F. Spray twelve 2½-inch muffin cups with cooking spray.

In a bowl, beat eggs, milk, Italian seasoning, salt, and black pepper until well blended. Add ham (if using), green onions, zucchini, red pepper, and ½ cup of the cheese; mix well.

Spoon about ¼ to ⅓ cup egg mixture into each cup. Sprinkle with remaining ½ cup cheese.

Bake just until eggs are set, about 20 to 22 minutes. Run a small knife around each cup. Let stand for 5 minutes.

**MAKE IT VEGAN**: Omit the ham. Use equivalent amount of a plant-based egg product in place of the eggs. Use plant-based cheese in place of the cheddar cheese.

**MAKE IT VEGETARIAN**: Omit the ham.

**ALLERGENS**: Dairy

EASY GLUTEN-FREE

# Ron's DIY Maple-Cracked Pepper Bacon

Ron's not invited to Galentine's Day brunch, but if he were, this spicy-sweet bacon is so good, he would ask for all of it.

---

**SERVES 6 TO 8**
**PREP TIME:** 5 MINUTES
**COOK TIME:** 20 MINUTES

**WHAT YOU NEED**
16 slices thick-cut bacon
6 tablespoons pure maple syrup
Cracked black pepper

**HOW YOU MAKE IT**
Preheat oven to 400°F. Line a 12-by-17-inch rimmed baking pan with foil. Place a wire rack in the pan. Arrange bacon slices on rack. Bake for 10 minutes.

Brush slices with maple syrup and sprinkle with pepper. Bake for 10 to 15 minutes more or until bacon is crisp.

**MAKE IT VEGAN OR VEGETARIAN:** Use plant-based bacon in place of the bacon. (It will not be gluten-free.)

# 'It's Raining Blood' Orange Salad

The murals of Pawnee are as legendary as they are offensive, but they do provide a valuable clue in Leslie's Valentine's Day riddle-fest for Ben. Mix up the first letters of all of the murals with a heart on them (including *"Cornfield Slaughter," "Lament of the Buffalo," "Needless Slaughter," "Slaughter Gone Wrong," "Eating the Reverend," "It's Raining Blood,"* and *"Death Everywhere"*), and what do you get? "No food finer. Clue three at JJ's Diner." This very fine winter citrus salad bursting with sweet and tart flavors pairs beautifully with waffles.

**SERVES 6 TO 8**

**PREP TIME:** 20 MINUTES

### WHAT YOU NEED

2 blood oranges, Cara Cara oranges, tangerines, or navel oranges, or a mix

3 clementines

2 small pink or ruby red grapefruit, or one of each

Kosher salt and freshly ground black pepper

1 shallot, very thinly sliced

6 tablespoons extra-virgin olive oil

2 tablespoons Champagne vinegar or white wine vinegar

1 teaspoon honey

2 teaspoons fresh lime juice

2 tablespoons minced fresh chives

### HOW YOU MAKE IT

Peel the oranges, clementines, and grapefruit, removing as much pith as possible. Slice into wheels. Remove any seeds and arrange on a serving platter. Season to taste with salt and pepper. Scatter shallot over the citrus.

In a small jar with a lid, combine olive oil, vinegar, honey, lime juice, and chives. Shake until well blended. Taste and adjust seasoning as needed.

Drizzle desired amount of dressing over the citrus.

**MAKE IT VEGAN:** Substitute pure maple syrup for the honey.

# Your Choice of German Muffin

Yvonne Clack, the cat-loving proprietress of The Quiet Corn bed and breakfast in Pawnee, likely would not have made these muffins so indulgent—they're moist and sweet, with a buttery streusel topping—but we did. Pick your perfect, sumptuous muffin—plain, poppy seed, apricot-almond, chocolate chip-dried cherry, or muesli. Enjoy with friends and skip the hard-boiled eggs, homemade tomato slices, and dry seed and leek jam.

**MAKES 12 MUFFINS**
**PREP TIME**: 15 MINUTES
**COOK TIME**: 18 MINUTES

### WHAT YOU NEED
Cooking spray
1¾ cups all-purpose flour
⅓ cup sugar
2 teaspoons baking powder
¼ teaspoon kosher salt
1 egg
¾ cup milk
¼ cup canola oil
1 recipe Streusel Topping

### HOW YOU MAKE IT
Preheat oven to 400°F. Spray twelve 2½-inch muffin cups with cooking spray or line with paper bake cups.

In a bowl, combine flour, sugar, baking powder, and salt. Make a well in center of flour mixture.

In another bowl, whisk together egg, milk, and oil. Add egg mixture all at once to flour mixture. Stir just until moistened (batter should be lumpy).

Spoon batter into prepared muffin cups, filling each two-thirds full. Sprinkle Streusel Topping over muffin batter in cups. Bake for 18 to 20 minutes or until golden and a wooden toothpick inserted in centers comes out clean. Cool in muffin cups on a wire rack for 5 minutes. Remove from muffin cups; serve warm.

**STREUSEL TOPPING**: In a small bowl, stir together 3 tablespoons flour, 3 tablespoons brown sugar, and ¼ teaspoon cinnamon. Cut in 2 tablespoons cold butter until the mixture resembles coarse crumbs. Stir in 2 tablespoons chopped pecans or walnuts.

**POPPY SEED MUFFINS**: Prepare as directed, except increase sugar to ½ cup and add 1 tablespoon poppy seeds to flour mixture.

**APRICOT-ALMOND MUFFINS**: Prepare as directed, except add ¾ cup finely chopped dried apricots and ½ teaspoon almond extract to batter. If adding Streusel Topping, substitute chopped almonds for the pecans or walnuts.

**CHOCOLATE CHIP-DRIED CHERRY MUFFINS**: Prepare as directed, except stir ½ cup each dried tart cherries and miniature semisweet chocolate chips into batter.

**MUESLI MUFFINS**: Prepare as directed, except reduce flour to 1⅓ cups and add ¾ cup muesli or rolled oats to flour mixture.

**MAKE IT GLUTEN-FREE**: Use a gluten-free flour blend in place of the all-purpose flour.

**MAKE IT VEGAN**: Use equivalent amount of a plant-based egg product in place of the egg. Substitute dairy butter and milk with plant-based butter and milk.

**ALLERGENS**: Wheat, dairy

EASY   GLUTEN-FREE   VEGETARIAN

# Lilith 'Fair Trade' Irish Coffee

You can make this sweet, creamy, and warming drink with any coffee, but if you want to take one small step to make the world a better place—like Leslie Knope does every day—look for a Fair Trade Certified bean. Fair Trade coffee is produced using rigorous standards that support farmers and their communities and help protect the environment.

**SERVES 1**
**PREP TIME:** 5 MINUTES

**WHAT YOU NEED**

Brown sugar

Strong, hot coffee

Good-quality Irish whiskey

Whipped cream

**HOW YOU MAKE IT**

For each drink, place 2 teaspoons packed brown sugar (or to taste) in a warm Irish coffee mug or other mug. Add 4 ounces hot coffee and 1½ ounces whiskey. Stir until sugar is dissolved. Top with whipped cream. (If you're a fan of tradition, don't stir. Drink the hot coffee through the whipped cream head.)

**MAKE IT VEGAN:** Use plant-based whipped cream in place of the dairy whipped cream.

**ALLERGENS:** Dairy

# Polka-Dot Balloon Bouquet

Leslie Knope has made the polka-dot balloon arch as iconic as Lucille Ball and Marilyn Monroe made the polka-dot dress. This balloon bouquet is simpler to make than an arch but creates the same festive effect.

## WHAT YOU NEED

Polka-dot balloons in red, pink, and white
Balloon sticks
Scissors
Small decorative watering can
2-inch-thick plastic foam, cut to fit container bottom
Washi tape in green pattern or florists tape
Ribbon

## HOW YOU MAKE IT

Blow up balloons to approximately the size of oranges or smaller; tie off. Place each balloon on a balloon stick. Trim each stick to the desired length.

Press the plastic foam piece into the bottom of the watering can.

Starting at the top of the balloon stick, wrap downward with washi or florists tape, stopping approximately 3 inches from the bottom.

Insert each stem into the foam, placing shorter stems around the edge and taller stems in the center.

Tie a ribbon bow around the handle of the watering can.

# Leslie's Dream Journal

*"We need a big, juicy idea. I'm so desperate, I even brought in my Dream Journal."* — Leslie Knope

Write down all of your big ideas and dreams in this inspiring, customizable journal. Or maybe just your dreams—even if they're as surreal as Leslie's "chipmunks dressed as waiters" or "teeny, tiny little burps that tasted like mints." Or give it to a friend so they can.

## WHAT YOU NEED

Ruler
Premade journal
Scissors
Decorative paper
Strong glue stick or hot glue
Printed inspirational messages
Stickers, iron-on trims, charms, string, or other assorted embellishments

### EQUIPMENT

Paper cutter
Computer
Printer

## HOW YOU MAKE IT

Measure the journal cover. Cut decorative paper slightly smaller than the cover. Use glue to attach the paper to the journal cover.

On a computer and using Word, place a blue text bubble shape on the document, making it approximately half the width of the journal cover. Add a text box over the bubble; type your favorite message in white as shown. Print the document. Trim the word bubble, leaving a narrow white border.

Arrange the embellishments on the cover until pleased with the design.

Working with one piece at a time, attach the embellishments using glue.

# Hand-Crocheted Flower Pens

To give a Leslie-level gift, pair Leslie's Dream Journal with these flower pens. And wrap them beautifully, of course.

## WHAT YOU NEED

Crochet hook (H8/5mm)

Cotton yarn in white, green, and desired flower colors

Scissors

Large-eyed embroidery needle

Pens

## HOW YOU MAKE IT

To crochet a flower, start with one strand of white yarn, chain seven. Skip two, and single crochet back through the chain around the end and up the other side. Continue working the pattern for one more round.

Tie in desired color and crochet another round. To make petal loops, chain three to six chains (three for short petals and up to six for longer petals) then connect back into crocheted round. Repeat until the center is surrounded with petals. Tie off the yarn and weave into the back side of the flower.

To make a leaf, chain seven using green yarn. Turn and single crochet in rounds along both sides until desired size is achieved. Tie off leaving long tails. Use the tails to stitch the leaf to the underside of the flower.

To add center details, thread a large-eyed embroidery needle with four strands of green yarn. Leaving long tails, make three large French knots in each flower center. Use the yarn tails to tie the crocheted flower to the pen top.

EASY

# Newspaper Headline Gift Bag

Marlene may have been less than enthused that Leslie's Galentine's Day gift of a needlepoint pillow featuring the headline from the day she was born happened to be *"Josef Stalin Dies,"* but it's the thought that counts. The headline on this gift bag may not be from the day your friend was born, but she'll still appreciate what's inside—even if it's not a needlepoint pillow with her face on it.

## WHAT YOU NEED
Ruler
Scissors
White paper gift bag
Newspaper or newspaper printouts from the internet
Glue stick
Ribbon
Tissue paper to coordinate with ribbon

## HOW YOU MAKE IT
Measure the front of the gift bag.

Trim newspaper or printout ¼ inch smaller, on each side, than the bag front.

Use glue stick to attach the cutout to the bag.

Tie a ribbon bow around the handle.

Wrap tissue paper around your gift and place in the bag.

# Gal Pal Acrostic Poems

*"Effervescent. He needs to be effervescent."* — Leslie Knope, revealing in a word puzzle what sort of bachelor the staff needs to help her find for Ann.

Be like Leslie—cleverly communicate your friends' most distinctive qualities in a keepsake acrostic poem.

## WHAT YOU NEED

White printer paper
Patterned cardstock cut to 3⅞-by-5⅛ inches
Glue stick
Small stickers that coordinate with cardstock
Colorful marking pens
Flat decorative bags, approximately 4½-by-6 inches
Decorated mini clothespins

## EQUIPMENT

Computer
Printer
Paper cutter

## HOW YOU MAKE IT

For each gal pal at the party, type their first name at the top of a 3¼-by-4¼-inch text box, leaving a ¼-inch margin on each side. (The example uses 28-pt Century Gothic font at the top and 18-pt Century Gothic for the individual letters and rules.) Below the name, type each letter, followed by underscores, on separate lines as shown in the photo.)

Add a colored border rule if desired.

Print copies of name cards for each guest at the party.

Using a paper cutter, trim a narrow border around each printout.

Use a glue stick to attach each trimmed printout to the center of a cardstock piece. Embellish with stickers, leaving the ruled area open.

During the party, give each guest cards for the other partygoers. Let them use marking pens to fill in words that describe that person, using the printed letters as starters for the acrostic activity.

Once all the cards are completed, take turns reading the fun things everyone wrote about each friend. Then separate the cards by name and let each guest take home their stack.

Offer small sacks to hold the cards, along with a mini clothespin to secure the sack closed.

# Sweet Crafternooner

*"Ron, I need a half-day off, for a secret mission of love."*
—Leslie Knope

*"You're asking my permission to take a nooner?"*
—Ron Swanson

When Leslie and Justin sought to reunite Marlene with Frank, they weren't headed off on THAT kind of nooner—and this isn't that kind either. This is an afternoon spent with friends, crafting and enjoying a selection of cookies, bars, chocolate fondue, and a refreshing, pretty-in-pink drink.

# 'The Bulge' Bars

On Valentine's Day, Pawnee's gay bar—The Bulge—is packed with revelers clubbing and looking for fun. Ron arrives looking for something else: a clue Leslie left there for Ben's scavenger hunt. Ron may not find his type of fun at The Bulge, but he does find the clue. The "bulges" in these nut-studded bars are stripes of rich, creamy vanilla buttercream covered with a blanket of decadent chocolate icing.

**MAKES 32 BARS**
**PREP TIME**: 1 HOUR
**COOK TIME**: 30 MINUTES

## WHAT YOU NEED

### FOR THE BARS

1 cup + 2 tablespoons butter
1¾ cups sugar
¾ cup unsweetened cocoa powder
3 large eggs
1½ teaspoons pure vanilla extract
2¼ cups all-purpose flour
1½ teaspoons baking powder
¼ teaspoon baking soda
1½ cups milk
1½ cups chopped cashews, almonds, walnuts, and/or pecans

### FOR THE VANILLA BUTTERCREAM

½ cup butter, softened
3 cups powdered sugar
3 tablespoons whole milk
½ teaspoon pure vanilla extract
⅛ teaspoon kosher salt

### FOR THE CHOCOLATE ICING

10 tablespoons butter
⅔ cup unsweetened cocoa powder
½ cup buttermilk
¼ cup dark corn syrup
⅛ teaspoon kosher salt
4 cups powdered sugar
½ teaspoon pure vanilla extract

## HOW YOU MAKE IT

**FOR THE BARS**: Preheat oven to 350°F. Grease a 9-by-13-inch baking pan. In a large microwave-safe bowl, microwave butter on high for 1½ to 2 minutes or until melted. Stir in sugar and cocoa powder until combined. Add eggs and vanilla. Using a wooden spoon, beat lightly just until combined.

In a small bowl, stir together flour, baking powder, and baking soda. Add flour mixture and milk alternately to chocolate mixture, beating after each addition. Stir in nuts.

Spread batter evenly in the prepared pan. Bake for 30 to 35 minutes or until a wooden toothpick inserted in the center comes out clean. Cool in the pan on a wire rack.

**FOR THE VANILLA BUTTERCREAM**: In a large bowl, beat butter with an electric mixer on medium speed for 1 minute. Add powdered sugar, milk, vanilla, and salt, and continue beating for 2 minutes more. Transfer to a piping bag fitted with a ½-inch round tip. Evenly pipe about 10 stripes of buttercream across the short side of the bars down the entire length of the bars, leaving a roughly 1-inch gap between stripes. Freeze bars, uncovered, until buttercream is very firm, about 1 hour.

**FOR THE CHOCOLATE ICING**: Melt butter in a pot over medium heat. Whisk in cocoa powder, buttermilk, corn syrup, and salt until well combined and bring to a rolling boil. Boil, whisking or stirring gently, for 2 minutes, then remove from heat and whisk in powdered sugar and vanilla

until smooth and silky. Let cool, stirring occasionally, until still warm and pourable but not hot, about 5 minutes.

Remove bars from the freezer and pour over the buttercream in wide, even ribbons to cover completely. (Don't use a knife—you want the icing to form valleys between the lines of buttercream rather than being flat on top.) If necessary, gently tip the pan side to side to distribute the icing.

Chill the bars in the refrigerator to let the icing set completely, about 1 hour, before cutting.

**MAKE IT GLUTEN-FREE:** Use a gluten-free flour blend in place of the all-purpose flour.

**MAKE IT VEGAN:** Substitute plant-based butter and milk for dairy butter and milk. Use equivalent amount of a plant-based egg product in place of the eggs. Substitute vegan buttermilk for the buttermilk.*

**\*NOTE:** To make vegan buttermilk, combine ½ cup plant-based milk with 1½ teaspoons lemon juice (or cider vinegar or white vinegar). Let stand 10 minutes.

**ALLERGENS:** Wheat, dairy, nuts

# Good Date Bars

*"You want a good date, why not ask out the
only guy that's made you smile tonight?"*
— April Ludgate, to Ann Perkins

While Tom and Ann's secret Valentine's Day date
pretty rapidly fell apart, he did get her to smile
and laugh more than anyone else at the dance.
They may not be a match made in heaven—but
the pairing of dates and pistachios in these
rich, crunchy, sweet, cardamom-infused bars
most certainly is.

**MAKES 24 BARS**
**PREP TIME**: 30 MINUTES
**COOK TIME**: 15 MINUTES

## WHAT YOU NEED

½ cup boiling water
⅓ cup snipped pitted whole dates
Cooking spray
½ cup all-purpose flour
½ teaspoon baking powder
¼ teaspoon ground cardamom
⅛ teaspoon baking soda
1 large egg
⅓ cup packed brown sugar
⅓ cup evaporated fat-free milk
2 tablespoons finely chopped toasted pistachios
2 tablespoons sifted powdered sugar

## HOW YOU MAKE IT

Preheat oven to 350°F. In a small bowl, combine
boiling water and dates. Cover and let stand for
10 minutes. Drain.

Coat an 8-by-8-by-2-inch baking pan with cooking spray;
set aside. In another bowl, whisk together flour, baking
powder, cardamom, and baking soda; set aside.

In a medium bowl, beat egg with an electric mixer on
high until frothy. Add brown sugar; beat until combined.
Stir in evaporated milk and drained dates.

Add flour mixture to egg mixture, stirring with a wooden
spoon until combined. Stir in pistachios. Pour batter into
the prepared baking pan.

Bake for 15 minutes or until a wooden toothpick inserted
near the center comes out clean. Cool in pan on a wire
rack. Sprinkle with powdered sugar. Cut into bars.

**MAKE IT GLUTEN-FREE**: Use a gluten-free flour blend
in place of the all-purpose flour.

**ALLERGENS**: Wheat, dairy, nuts

# April's Secretly Sincere Chocolate Hugs Cookies

*"When I started working for you, I was aimless and just thought everything was stupid and lame—and you turned me into someone with goals and ambition— which is really the only reason why I'm even thinking about what I really want. And I just want to say thank you. And I love you very much. Which is why I have decided not to turn you into a sea urchin, which I could do, because I am an actual witch with powers, and I am evil, and I hate everything."* — April Ludgate

These rich, fudgy cookies hug the crème-striped candies a bit like April hugs Leslie in their heart-to-heart in Washington, D.C.

**MAKES ABOUT 50 COOKIES**
**PREP TIME:** 45 MINUTES
**COOK TIME:** 10 MINUTES

## WHAT YOU NEED

1¾ cups all-purpose flour
¾ cup unsweetened cocoa powder
½ teaspoon baking soda
½ teaspoon kosher salt
½ cup butter, softened
¾ cup packed brown sugar
½ cup granulated sugar, plus more for sprinkling
2½ teaspoons pure vanilla extract
2 large eggs
Hershey's Hugs Kisses, wrappers removed

## HOW YOU MAKE IT

Preheat oven to 350°F. Line two cookie sheets with parchment paper.

In a bowl, whisk together flour, cocoa powder, baking soda, and salt.

In a stand mixer fitted with the paddle attachment, combine butter, brown sugar, the ½ cup granulated sugar, and the vanilla. Beat on medium until light and fluffy. Add eggs and beat until well blended, scraping sides of bowl as needed. Add the flour mixture and mix on low just until ingredients are well combined.

Roll dough into 1-inch balls. Roll in granulated sugar and place on prepared cookie sheets. Bake for 10 to 12 minutes or just until cookies are puffed and starting to crack. Do not overbake.

Remove cookies from the oven and immediately press a Hershey's Hug into the middle of each cookie. Remove cookies to a wire rack and cool completely.

**MAKE IT GLUTEN-FREE:** Use a gluten-free flour blend in place of the all-purpose flour.
**ALLERGENS:** Wheat, dairy, soy

# 'You Just Got Jammed!' Thumbprint Cookies

*"Tom, do you want to know why I moved to Pawnee? It's because the two leading industries here are corn syrup and rubber nipples. It's a dentistry jackpot. It's genius, right?"* — Jeremy Jamm

These buttery, nut-crusted cookies are their own kind of genius—simple to make but pretty and full of strawberry flavor. Look for a jam without corn syrup—and be sure to brush your teeth after indulging in sweets of any kind. Visits to the dentist are not particularly fun—even if you happen to have a nice, normal one.

**MAKES ABOUT 30 COOKIES**
**PREP TIME**: 30 MINUTES + 1 HOUR CHILLING
**COOK TIME**: 10 MINUTES

### WHAT YOU NEED

⅔ cup butter, softened
½ cup sugar
2 eggs, separated
1 teaspoon pure vanilla extract
1½ cups all-purpose flour
1 cup finely chopped almonds or walnuts
Strawberry jam

### HOW YOU MAKE IT

In a bowl, beat butter with an electric mixer on medium for 30 seconds. Add sugar. Beat until combined, scraping sides of bowl as needed. Beat in egg yolks and vanilla until combined. Beat in flour. Chill, covered, 1 hour or until dough is easy to handle.

Preheat oven to 375°F. Line a cookie sheet with parchment paper. Shape dough into 1-inch balls. Lightly beat egg whites. Roll dough balls in egg whites, then roll in chopped nuts. Place balls 1 inch apart on prepared cookie sheet. Using your thumb, make an indent in the center of each ball.

Bake 10 to 12 minutes or until bottoms are light brown. (If the centers of the cookies puff up during baking, press with the round side of a measuring teaspoon.) Let cool completely on a wire rack.

Just before serving, fill the center of each cookie with ½ teaspoon strawberry jam.

**MAKE IT GLUTEN-FREE**: Use a gluten-free flour blend in place of the all-purpose flour.

**MAKE IT VEGAN**: Use equivalent amount of a plant-based egg product in place of the eggs. Substitute plant-based butter for the dairy butter.

**ALLERGENS**: Wheat, dairy, nuts

# Chocolate Fountain Fondue

Other than heart-shaped balloon arches and Mouse Rat—LIVE!—what could make the Valentine's Dance at the Pawnee Senior Center even better? Warm, velvety, decadent chocolate fondue, of course. It's all the fun of a chocolate fountain without the mess and rental fee.

**SERVES 8**
**PREP TIME:** 15 MINUTES

**WHAT YOU NEED**

8 ounces semisweet chocolate, coarsely chopped

1 (14-ounce) can sweetened condensed milk

⅓ cup whole milk

Assorted dippers, such as strawberries; sliced kiwi; sliced pear; angel food cake or pound cake cubes; mandarin orange segments; and/or pretzels (waffle shape if you can find them!); and dried apricots, papaya, and/or mango

**HOW TO MAKE IT**

In a medium heavy pot, melt chocolate over medium heat, stirring frequently. Stir in sweetened condensed milk and whole milk; heat through. Transfer to a fondue pot; keep warm.

Serve fondue with dippers.

**NOTE:** If the fondue thickens, stir in additional milk.

**CHOCOLATE-LIQUEUR FONDUE:** Stir 2 to 4 tablespoons amaretto, orange, hazelnut, or cherry liqueur into mixture after heating.

**MOCHA FONDUE:** Substitute ⅓ cup strong brewed coffee for the milk.

**ALLERGENS:** Dairy, soy

EASY GLUTEN-FREE VEGAN

# Ann's Effervescent Wine Spritzer

What does Leslie demand of any eligible bachelor good enough for Ann? He has to be Educated, Friendly, Fun, Egalitarian, Robust, Vigorous, Enthusiastic, Sexy, Courteous, Empathetic, definitely Not Pigeon-Toed, and Talented. Oh, and effervescent. He needs to be effervescent. Bubbly and pretty in pink, this light, refreshing beverage is the perfect sipper for an afternoon of crafting with your gal pals.

**SERVES 1**
**PREP TIME:** 5 MINUTES

**WHAT YOU NEED**

Dry rosé wine, chilled

Pink grapefruit juice, chilled

Ice cubes

Club soda, chilled

Fresh thyme sprig

Fresh raspberries

**HOW YOU MAKE IT**

For each drink, combine 4 ounces rosé and 2 ounces grapefruit juice in a Collins, highball, or wine glass over ice. Top off with club soda. Rub the thyme sprig between your fingers to release the oils. Add to the drink and use as a swizzle stick to stir. Garnish with fresh raspberries.

**MAKE IT A MOCKTAIL:** Omit wine. Use 6 ounces grapefruit juice and add additional club soda.

# Sweetums Candy Bar

*"If sugar is so bad, how come Jesus made it taste so good?"* — Pawnee resident

Fill the jars of this *"candy bar"* with Sweetums favorites such as Nuts 'N' Stuf, Teef Killers, and Kandy Nailz—or make up your own names—just none of that healthy NutriYums stuff.

## WHAT YOU NEED

Decorative glass jars
White printer paper
Scissors
Strong double-sided tape
Decorative ribbon
Assorted candies

## HOW YOU MAKE IT

For each candy jar, print a fun name on white paper to describe the candy using the photo for inspiration. (These labels are 1 inch high and are as long as needed.) Trim around the name.

Use double-sided tape to adhere each label to a glass jar.

Tie a ribbon bow around each jar knob; trim ribbon ends.

Fill each jar with candy.

# Mosaic Portraits

If you don't have the time and patience to crush enough diet soda bottles to make the pieces for these mosaic portraits—like Leslie did for her friends—squares of tissue paper make a fine substitute.

## WHAT YOU NEED

White printer paper

12-inch square of Baltic birch

Ballpoint pen

Black marking pen

Tissue paper in desired colors/prints for skin, eyes, lips, clothing, jewelry, and hair

Paintbrush

White glue

Pencil with eraser

## EQUIPMENT

Printer/copier

## HOW YOU MAKE IT

Print or copy a friend's portrait photo, enlarging if necessary to make it approximately 9 inches tall.

Place the printout centered on the piece of Baltic birch. Using a ballpoint pen and heavy pressure, trace the portrait outline and basic details. Remove the paper. Retrace the etched lines using a marking pen.

Tear the paper for the skin, eyes, and lips into tiny pieces. Working in small facial areas at a time, brush on white glue. Press the appropriate pieces on the glue, cutting or tearing at the edges of the drawn outlines and leaving small spaces between pieces to expose some of the wood underneath. Continue working in this manner until the face is complete.

For clothing and jewelry, cut paper into 1-inch squares. Continue to work in small areas; brush on glue. Place the pencil eraser in the center of a tissue paper square, twist, and place onto glue; remove pencil. Continue in this manner until each area is filled. Let the glue dry.

For hair, use the same method as for the clothing. Or, as shown here, cut various-width strips from tissue paper. Tack the top ends down by placing glue on the wood; press ends in place. Twist strips as desired and tack ends in the same manner. Fill in areas as needed with twisted squares of tissue paper.

# Galentine's Snow Globe

*"It's Valentine's Day, and I'm working the late shift at the Snow Globe Museum, so I'm right where I want to be." — Kevin*

While Kevin may not be having the best Valentine's Day, you can make someone's day a little more magical with this fun and unique gift. With minimal supplies and just a few minutes, you can craft a snow globe as enchanting as any displayed at the Hompherman Snow Globe Museum.

## WHAT YOU NEED

Coarse sandpaper

Jar with lid

Mini fairy garden or valentine decorations in plastic or ceramic material (metal can rust)

Clear epoxy

Water

Glitter in silver or white

Glycerin

## HOW YOU MAKE IT

Sand the inside of the jar lid to roughen the surface.

Arrange the decoration(s) on the inside of the jar lid, making sure the items fit so the lid can screw onto the jar with ease. Glue decoration(s) in place with clear epoxy; let dry.

Fill the jar almost to the top with water; add a shake or two of glitter and only just a few drops of glycerin to avoid making the glitter clumpy.

Carefully screw on the lid tightly without disturbing the decoration.

# 'Ovaries before Brovaries' Cross-Stitch Napkins

*"You know my code: Hoes before bros. Uteruses before duderuses. Ovaries before brovaries."* — Leslie Knope

Declare your allegiance to sisterhood while providing a thoroughly practical means of holding a glass that's slippery and wet from condensation. (They make a pretty fabulous party favor, too.)

**WHAT YOU NEED**
Evenweave napkins
Embroidery floss in red, periwinkle, and pink
Embroidery needle
Red pom-pom trim
Red thread

**EQUIPMENT**
Sewing machine

**HOW YOU MAKE IT**
Using the pattern below, cross-stitch a corner of the napkin, leaving a ½-inch border at the bottom and side. Add backstitches and lazy daisy stitches.

Machine-stitch the pom-pom trim around the edge.

# Homemade Valentines for Your Gal Pal

*"Oh, Ann, you beautiful tropical fish."* — Leslie Knope

Nothing conveys your love and admiration for your BFF like a homemade valentine declaring her a "Poetic Noble Land Mermaid," a "Rainbow-Infused Space Unicorn," a "Beautiful, Rule-Breaking Moth"—or any other weird, one-of-a-kind phrase of praise you can come up with.

## WHAT YOU NEED (FOR EACH VALENTINE)

3½-by-4¾-inch piece of white cardstock

Colored marking pens

Embroidery needle

White glue

Variegated embroidery floss in desired colors

3¾-by-5-inch colored cardstock to coordinate with design

4¼-by-5½-inch blank card and envelope in color of choice

## EQUIPMENT

Copier

## HOW YOU MAKE IT

Using the patterns (below) and the photo (opposite) as a guide, write the desired message on the white cardstock using marking pens, leaving room for the desired stitched design.

Copy the pattern that corresponds to the message; trim around image.

On a protected surface, place the pattern on the white cardstock where desired. Using the embroidery needle, poke dots around the pattern.

Using embroidery floss, stitch the design using backstitches through the poked holes.

Glue the finished message centered on coordinating colored cardstock, then glue cardstock centered on the front of the blank card. Let dry before placing in envelope.

**ENLARGE 150%**

# Treat Yo Self

*"Three words for you: Treat. Yo. Self."*
—Tom Haverford

Treating yourself can mean different things to different people. For Donna and Tom, it's clothes, fragrances, massages, mimosas, fine leather goods, and "sushi made from fish previously owned by celebrities." For Ben, well, it's a superhero suit. Establish your own Treat Yo Self Day with these spa-style delicacies and pampering self-care goodies.

# 'Beautiful, Talented, Brilliant, Powerful Musk Ox' Mimosa Bar

*"Ann, you are such a good friend. You're a beautiful, talented, brilliant, powerful musk ox." — Leslie Knope*

A beautiful, customizable self-serve mimosa bar is a brilliant idea for a spa day with friends. After all, Treat Yo Self is a day all about indulging in the luxuries you love the most.

**SERVINGS VARY**

**PREP TIME:** 30 MINUTES

## WHAT YOU NEED

### FOR SERVING

Blank wooden tags (enough for the number of juices you are serving)

Twine or ribbon

Ice bucket and ice

Inexpensive glass beverage carafes (enough for the number of juices you are serving)

Platter and small tongs for serving garnishes

Collins or highball glasses, or Champagne flutes or other stemmed glassware

### FOR THE BEVERAGES

Variety of chilled sparkling wines, such as Champagne, Cava, sparkling rosé, and/or prosecco

Variety of chilled juices, such as orange, tangerine, grapefruit, pineapple, pomegranate, and/or peach or apricot nectar

Selection of liqueurs, such as crème de cassis (black currant), Chambord (raspberry), Cointreau (orange), limoncello (lemon), and/or kirsch (cherry) (optional)

Garnishes, such as fresh raspberries and/or blackberries; pomegranate seeds; halved strawberries; lemon, orange, and lime slices; edible flowers such as borage, nasturtium, violas, or unsprayed rose petals; and/or fresh herbs such as mint or basil leaves, or lavender, rosemary, or thyme sprigs

## HOW YOU MAKE IT

Use the wooden tags and alphabet stickers to create labels identifying the types of juices you are serving. Thread with twine or ribbon, and tie around the necks of the beverage carafes.

When you are ready to serve, fill the ice bucket with ice. Place sparkling wine selections on ice to keep chilled. Decant the chilled juices into the carafes. Arrange garnishes on a serving platter. Line up mimosa bar elements in the following order: Glasses, ice bucket, liqueurs, juices, sparkling wines, and garnishes.

For one drink, pour a splash of desired liqueur (if using) into a glass over ice. Add equal parts desired juice and sparkling wine. Top with desired garnishes.

**MAKE IT A MOCKTAIL:** Substitute chilled club soda or tonic water for the sparkling wine.

# Platter of Crudité from 'The Pit' with VIP D-I-P

*"Somebody just planted a garden down there with fruits and vegetables, so I'm getting a lot of vitamins."* — Andy Dwyer

Andy's residence in *"The Pit"* may have lacked luxury, but he did have an array of fresh produce to pick from once Leslie established the community garden. This crudité platter features carrots with trimmed tops—and lots of other vitamin-packed veggies, too—served with a tangy, creamy, superstar caramelized onion-sour cream dip.

**SERVES 6 TO 8**
**PREP TIME:** 30 MINUTES + 1 HOUR CHILLING
**COOK TIME:** 15 MINUTES

## WHAT YOU NEED

**FOR THE DIP**
2 tablespoons olive oil
1 large onion, chopped
3 large shallots, chopped
2 teaspoons sugar
1 teaspoon kosher salt
4 cloves garlic, minced
1½ cups light sour cream
⅔ cup light mayonnaise
2 tablespoons minced fresh chives
¼ teaspoon freshly ground black pepper

**FOR THE CRUDITÉ:**
Small slender carrots, tops trimmed (leave some green), peeled
Radishes, halved if desired
Grape, cherry, or pear tomatoes (red, yellow, or orange, or a mix)
Sugar snap peas, blanched*
Cauliflower and/or broccoli florets, or Broccolini
Persian cucumbers (also called mini cucumbers), sliced on the diagonal
Multicolor mini bell peppers, halved, stems left on

## HOW YOU MAKE IT

**FOR THE DIP:** In a large skillet, heat oil over medium heat. Add onion, shallots, sugar, and ½ teaspoon salt, and stir to combine. Reduce heat to medium-low. Cook and stir until onion and shallots are golden, about 15 to 20 minutes. Remove from heat; cool. Stir in garlic.

In a medium bowl, stir together the cooled onion mixture, sour cream, mayonnaise, chives, remaining ½ teaspoon salt, and the pepper. Cover and chill 1 hour to blend flavors. (Dip can be made 24 hours ahead. Take out of the refrigerator 20 minutes before serving.)

**FOR THE CRUDITÉ:** Arrange the vegetables on a large serving platter.

Transfer dip to a serving bowl. Serve with crudité.

**\*NOTE:** To blanch the snap peas, bring a pot of water to a boil. Add snap peas. Cook for 30 seconds to 1 minute. Scoop out with a slotted spoon and immediately plunge into a bowl of ice water to stop the cooking process. Drain.

**MAKE IT VEGAN:** Use vegan sour cream and vegan mayonnaise in place of the dairy sour cream and mayo.

**ALLERGENS:** Dairy

# Leslie's Super-Intense Chocolate Truffles

*"You love harder than anyone I know, and it's tough to match."* — Ann Perkins, to Leslie Knope

Leslie loves to give gifts—and not just any old store-bought thing. Forget the boxed candies from the chocolate shop. Show your besties how much you love them, Leslie style, with these rich, velvety, and very special truffles you make yourself.

**MAKES 25 TO 30 TRUFFLES**

**PREP TIME**: 1 HOUR + 1½ HOURS CHILLING

**COOK TIME**: 10 MINUTES

## WHAT YOU NEED

12 ounces bittersweet chocolate, finely chopped

⅓ cup heavy cream

4 teaspoons cherry brandy, hazelnut or orange liqueur, or milk

3 tablespoons finely chopped candied cherries or candied orange peel

Unsweetened cocoa powder; very finely chopped pistachios, toasted; finely shredded coconut; very finely crushed freeze-dried strawberries or raspberries; and/or powdered sugar

## HOW YOU MAKE IT

In a medium heavy pot, combine chocolate and heavy cream. Cook and stir constantly over low heat until chocolate melts, about 10 minutes. Remove saucepan from heat; cool slightly. Sir in cherry brandy. Beat mixture with an electric mixer on low speed until smooth. Stir in cherries. Chill until firm, 1½ to 2 hours.

Line a tray or baking sheet with parchment paper. Using your hands, roll and shape chilled chocolate mixture into ¾- to 1-inch balls and place on prepared pan (a 1-inch cookie dough scoop works well). (If the ganache gets too warm, put it back in the refrigerator to firm up.) Roll balls in cocoa powder, pistachios, coconut, crushed freeze-dried strawberries or raspberries, and/or powdered sugar, and place on prepared pan.

Store in a single layer in an airtight container in the refrigerator for up to 2 weeks. Let stand at room temperature about 30 minutes before serving.

**MAKE IT VEGAN**: Use plant-based heavy cream in place of the dairy heavy cream.

**ALLERGENS**: Dairy, soy

# Unicorn Cupcakes

*"Ann, you rainbow-infused space unicorn."* — Leslie Knope

These rainbow-striped, bejeweled, and glittery treats are as sweet as the sincerest compliment you could give your best friend, even if it's also the weirdest.

---

**MAKES 24 CUPCAKES**

**PREP TIME:** 45 MINUTES

**COOK TIME:** 20 MINUTES

## WHAT YOU NEED

### FOR THE CUPCAKES

Paper bake cups in unicorn design or pastel colors (pink, purple, green, orange, yellow, blue)

1 (15.25-ounce) box white cake mix

1¼ cups Champagne or other dry sparkling wine, room temperature

⅓ cup vegetable oil

3 large egg whites

4 or 5 drops red food coloring

### FOR THE FROSTING

½ cup butter, softened

4 cups powdered sugar

¼ cup Champagne or other dry sparkling wine, room temperature

1 teaspoon pure vanilla extract

Paste or gel food coloring (pink, purple, green, orange, yellow, blue)

Desired decorations: Iridescent multicolor candy sprinkles; small gold and pearl dragees; rainbow jimmies; and/or rainbow sanding sugar

24 edible unicorn horn and ear decorations, such as Wilton® brand

## HOW YOU MAKE IT

**FOR THE CUPCAKES:** Preheat oven to 350°F. Line a twenty-four 2½-inch muffin cups with paper bake cups.

In a large bowl, stir together cake mix and Champagne. Add oil, egg whites, and food coloring to make a pink batter. Beat with an electric mixer on medium speed for 2 minutes. Divide among bake cups. Bake as directed on box for cupcakes. Cool completely on a wire rack.

**FOR THE FROSTING:** In a medium bowl, beat butter, powdered sugar, Champagne, and vanilla with electric mixer on medium speed until smooth. Evenly divide frosting among three bowls. Tint each with one desired color of paste or gel food coloring.

When cupcakes have cooled completely, spoon each of the three colors into one side of a large pastry bag fitted with a large star tip, being careful not to mix frostings in the bag. Pipe frosting onto cupcakes, swirling in a circle as you work. Sprinkle with desired decorations. Top with unicorn horn and ear decorations.

**MAKE IT GLUTEN-FREE:** Use a gluten-free cake mix in place of the regular cake mix.

**MAKE IT VEGAN:** Use equivalent amount of a plant-based egg product in place of the egg whites. Use plant-based butter in place of the dairy butter.

**ALLERGENS:** Wheat, dairy

# 'Fine Leather Goods' Napkin Rings

On the *"best day of the year,"* Donna and Tom spend a day treating themselves to clothes, fragrances, massages, mimosas, and Fine. Leather. Goods. These handmade leather napkin rings will bring style and flair to any table setting.

## WHAT YOU NEED

6½-by-2-inch pieces of firm colored leather

Ruler

Marking pen

Cutting board

Hammer

Awl

Sewing needle

Heavy-duty thread

Small wood beads to contrast with leather

Button

## HOW YOU MAKE IT

Using a ruler, make a mark on the right side of the leather piece (¼ inch from the edge) every ½ inch along both long edges. On each short end, make two or four holes (depending on button), centered top to bottom.

Place the leather strip on a protected surface, such as a cutting board. Hammer the awl through each marked dot, leaving small holes.

Sew beads along each long edge.

On one short end, sew an elastic loop on one side. Sew the button on the opposite end.

Overlap the short ends; secure by sewing on the button. If it is too tricky to sew the button through both layers, attach it to just one and hot-glue the leather strip into a ring.

# Tom's 'Never Stop Dreaming' Tie-Dyed Pillowcase

Tom Haverford may be a not-so-successful serial entrepreneur, but you've got to admire his optimism. His premier entertainment conglomerate Entertainment 7Twenty may have been a very expensive bust, but he'll never stop dreaming about his next venture—and you don't have to, either. Lay your head on this softly colored pillowcase to get some good sleep—which just might lead to an outlook as relentlessly positive as Tom's.

**WHAT YOU NEED**

White pillowcase
Rubber bands or cable ties
Pastel tie-dye kit
Gold fabric marking pen

**HOW YOU MAKE IT**

Following the tie-dye kit instructions, fold, twist, pleat, scrunch, or shape the pillowcase as desired; secure the design with rubber bands or cable ties if needed.

Following the instructions on the tie-dye kit, dye the pillowcase. Dry and set the dye according to the dye manufacturer, removing rubber bands or cable ties as directed.

Using a gold fabric marking pen, write "Never Stop Dreaming" on one corner of the pillowcase. Let the ink dry.

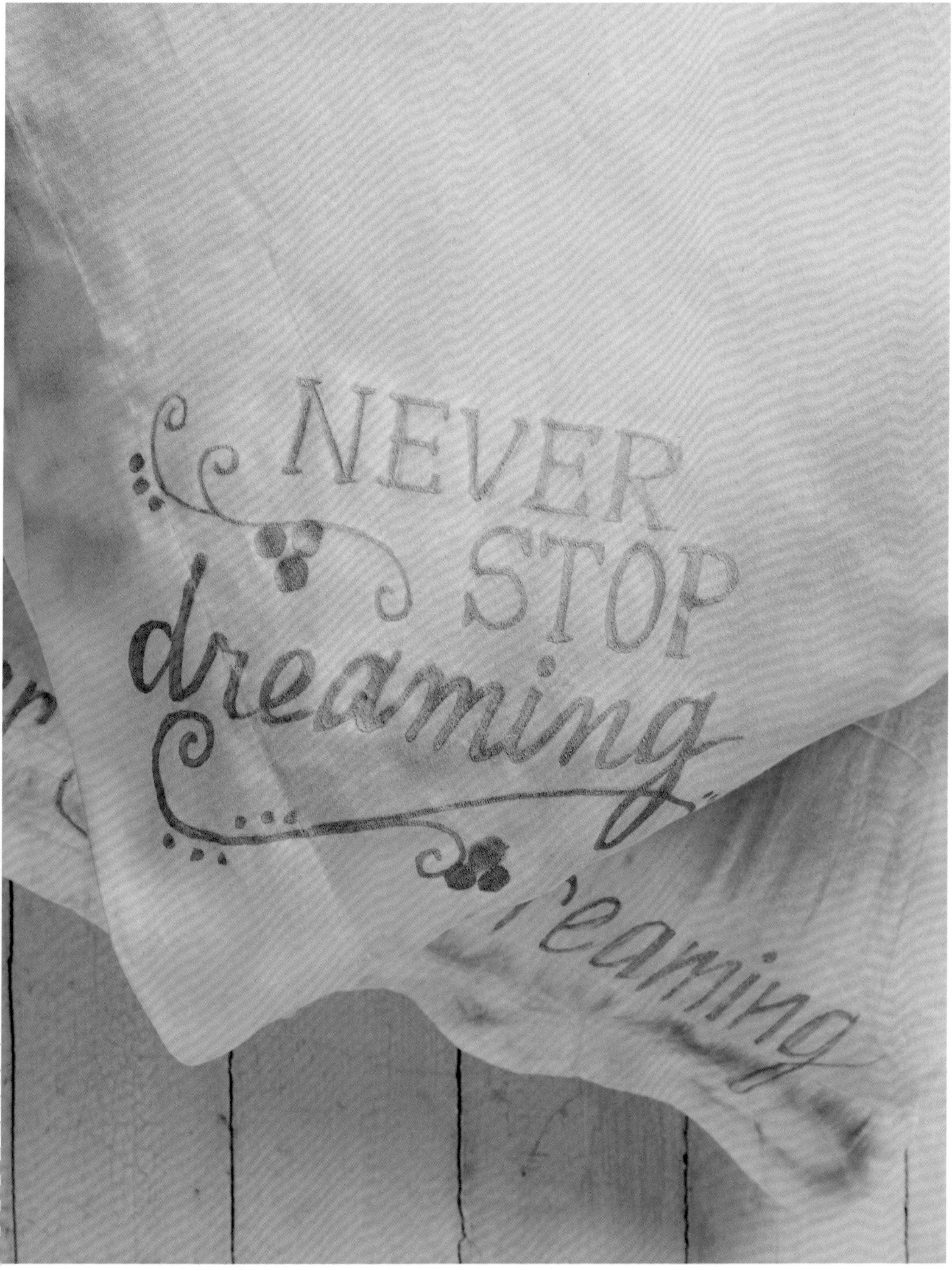
NEVER
STOP
dreaming

# DIY Eye Masks

*"Relaxation lesson Number 1: Acupuncture. It's great for your legs and your rear. Needles in your face, pleasure in your base."* — Donna Meagle

These lavender-scented eye masks will provide pleasure on your face—not in your base—by hydrating your eyes and skin while filling your nose with a lovely lavender aroma. Warm them slightly in the microwave, lay them over your eyes, and, in the words of Tom Haverford, "Just relaaaax, man."

## WHAT YOU NEED

**Cotton fabric**
**Scissors**
**Straight pins**
**Matching thread**
**Dried rice**
**Dried lavender buds**
**Quilt labels**

## EQUIPMENT

**Sewing machine**

## HOW YOU MAKE IT

Using the pattern (below), cut a front, back, and two lining pieces from cotton fabric.

Place the front and back pieces right sides facing. Sandwich the layers between two lining pieces; pin.

Stitch the layers together using a ¼-inch seam, leaving a 1-inch opening at the top to turn. Clip the curves; turn right-side out.

Fill the pouch with rice and lavender.

Hand-sew the opening closed. Stitch a quilt label to the upper right corner of the eye mask.

To use, heat in the microwave for 30 to 45 seconds or until just warm. (Do not overheat!) Place over eyes.

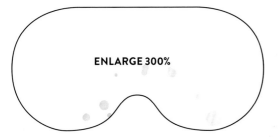

ENLARGE 300%

# DIT 'Yearning' Perfume by Dennis Feinstein

*"Mr. Feinstein, Tom Haverford. I'm the organizer of this soirée, and I'm also a huge fan of yours. I use all your colognes. Sometimes two at once!"* — Tom Haverford

This choose-your-own adventure in perfumery allows you to custom-blend your own brand of Yearning. You'll smell good in the exact way you want to—and when you smell good, you feel good.

## WHAT YOU NEED

100-proof alcohol, such as vodka

Essential oils in desired scents

White printer paper or colored printer paper

Small decorative bottles with corks

Decorative-edge scissors

Double-sided tape

Trims to coordinate with perfume scents, such as pinecones, faux flowers, beads, etc.

Narrow ribbon

## EQUIPMENT

Printer

Hot-glue gun

## HOW YOU MAKE IT

Fill each bottle ¼ full with vodka

Referring to the internet for inspiration, add essential oils in desired combinations.

Design and print a label for each bottle creating a fun name relating to each scent. Cut out the label using decorative-edge scissors. Adhere the label to the bottle using double-sided tape.

Use hot glue to attach tiny decorations to the cork. Tie a narrow ribbon bow around the jar neck.

midsummer
bloom
almond-enhanced
lavender

the
wild side
fir-spiked
peppermint

sweet
&
zesty
cinnamon-induced
orange

# 'I Love Amenities!' Gift Bag

Tom Haverford's lush lifestyle—witnessed by Ann and Leslie on a secret tour of his apartment—may have put him deeply in debt, but you won't have to spend much other than a little time to make and give these customizable gift bags. Fill with boutique eye cream, unisex cologne, lip exfoliator, and chocolate-covered almonds—or whatever little luxuries you like.

## WHAT YOU NEED (FOR 1 BAG)

24-by-9½-inch piece of print fabric
Straight pins
24-by-9½-inch piece of solid fabric for lining
Matching sewing thread
Scissors
Small safety pin
¼-inch ribbon
Iron-on initials
Assorted toiletries, slippers, bath accessories, etc.

## EQUIPMENT

Sewing machine
Iron

## HOW YOU MAKE IT

Fold print fabric with right sides and short ends together; pin.

Using ½-inch seam allowances, machine-stitch along each side; turn.

Stitch lining piece in the same manner; do not turn.

Trim seams. Tuck lining into outer bag. Fold down a ¼-inch cuff. Fold again and top-stitch to hold in place.

Personalize the front with iron-on initials. Follow the manufacturer's instructions to adhere.

Hand-tack the center of an 18-inch-long piece of ¼-inch-wide ribbon to the left side seam, 1½ inches from the top. Fill with amenities; tie closed using the ribbon.

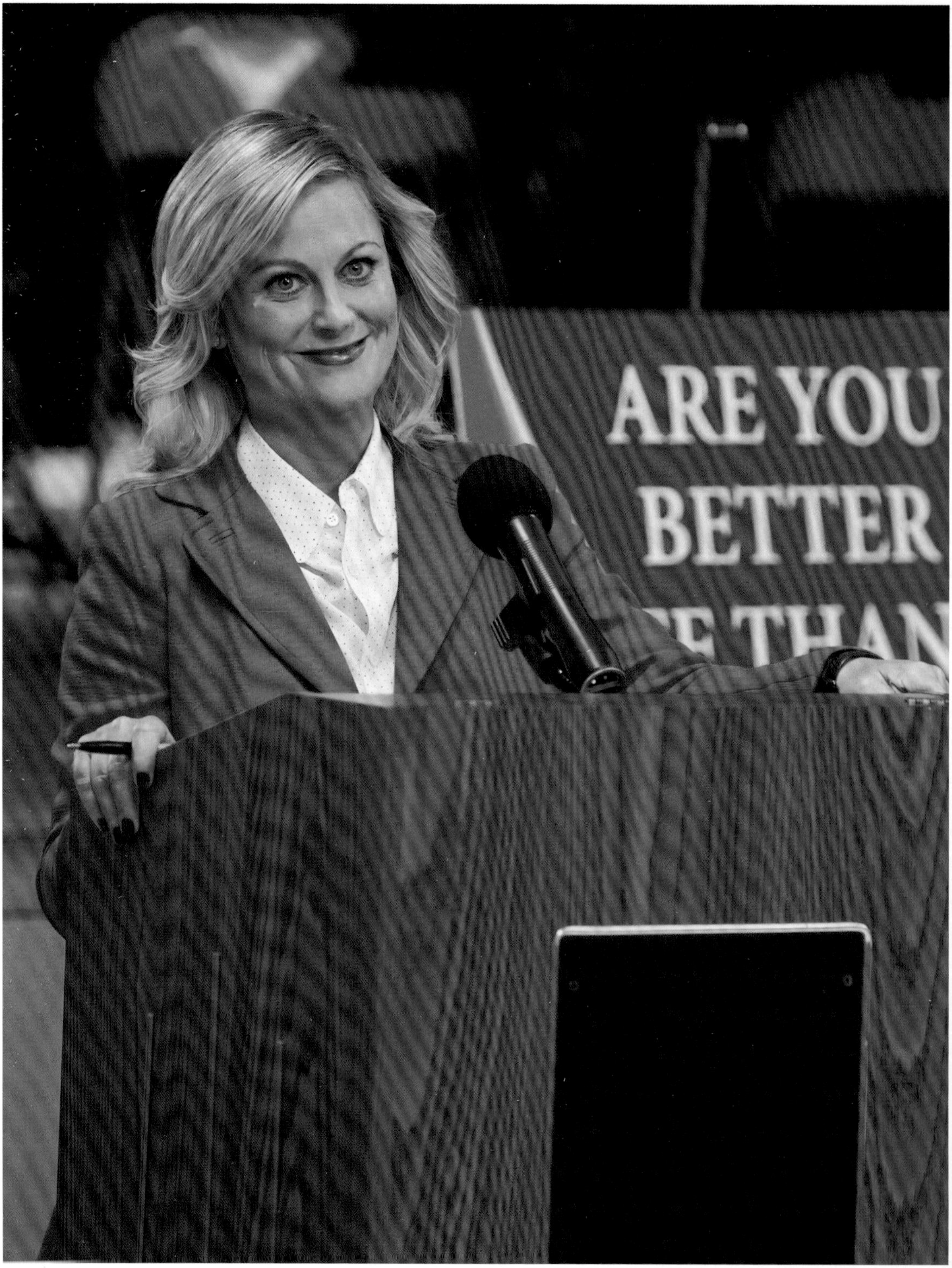
ARE YOU
BETTER

# Heroines' Tea

*"Maybe it's time for more women to be in charge."*
—Leslie Knope

Honor the strong, smart, powerful women who have made history (and earned a spot in Leslie Knope's pantheon of heroines) with a gathering of strong, smart, powerful gal pals. Dress up in a power blazer and pearls (or as one of your own female role models!) to sip tea, nibble on sandwiches and cookies—and talk about how to take over the world. Pinkies up!

# Strong-as-a-Woman Spiced Tea

*"A woman is like a tea bag. You never know how strong it is until it's in hot water."*
— Eleanor Roosevelt

Leslie may have narrowly (and drunkenly) escaped getting a "tastefully done" tattoo of the former first lady on the night of the recall vote, but that doesn't dampen her enthusiasm for the legendary human rights leader. This cinnamon-and-clove-spiced tea flavored with orange zest and honey is—like Roosevelt and all who emulate her—robust and energizing.

**SERVES 8**
**PREP TIME:** 5 MINUTES
**COOK TIME:** 10 MINUTES

## WHAT YOU NEED

½ cup black tea leaves, such as Assam or Ceylon

2 tablespoons whole cloves

3 tablespoons orange or tangerine zest

4 whole cinnamon sticks

Cheesecloth

100% cotton kitchen twine

2 quarts water

½ cup honey

¼ cup fresh lemon juice

Whole milk (optional)

## HOW YOU MAKE IT

Cut a double thickness of cheesecloth into an 8-by-8-inch square. Place the tea, cloves, orange zest, and cinnamon sticks in the center. Draw up the corners and tie into a bag with twine. Trim off the top a bit if necessary.

In a medium pot with a lid, bring water to a boil. Add cheesecloth bag, remove from heat, and let steep, covered, for 10 minutes. Remove and discard the bag. Stir in honey and lemon juice.

Ladle hot tea into a teapot to serve, heating remaining tea and refilling tea pot as needed. Serve with milk (if using).

# April's Dinosaur-Shape Tea Sandwiches

*"Last week he was supposed to buy gas, but instead he bought novelty cookie cutters. Now everything we eat is shaped like a dinosaur. He's amazing."* — April Ludgate

It's a good thing for Andy and April that they have the same quirky take on life. Aside from their unconventional shapes, though, these petite sandwiches are anything but off the wall. Three classic fillings—delicate cucumber-dill, peppery watercress-butter, and savory curried egg salad—are all perfect paired with a cup of hot tea.

## SERVES 6 (EACH SANDWICH TYPE)

### WHAT YOU NEED

**FOR CUCUMBER-DILL SANDWICHES**

4 ounces cream cheese, softened

1 teaspoon lemon zest

1 teaspoon chopped fresh dill

Pinch kosher salt

6 slices soft white sandwich bread

½ English cucumber

**FOR WATERCRESS-BUTTER SANDWICHES**

4 tablespoons butter, softened

½ teaspoon lemon zest

1 tablespoon minced fresh chives

Pinch kosher salt

6 slices soft white sandwich bread

1 cup watercress leaves

**FOR CURRIED EGG SALAD SANDWICHES**

3 hard-boiled eggs, finely chopped

3 tablespoons finely chopped celery

3 tablespoons finely chopped red onion

3 tablespoons chopped fresh cilantro

2 teaspoons Dijon mustard

2 teaspoons fresh lime juice

¼ cup mayonnaise

½ teaspoon curry powder

Pinch kosher salt

6 slices soft white sandwich bread

3 tablespoons mango chutney

### HOW TO MAKE IT

**FOR THE CUCUMBER-DILL SANDWICHES:** In a bowl, stir together cream cheese, lemon zest, dill, and salt. Spread one side of each bread slice with cream cheese mixture. Cut the cucumber into paper-thin slices and arrange over cream cheese on 3 of the bread slices. Top with remaining bread slices, cream cheese side down. Cut each whole sandwich into 2 sandwiches with dinosaur-shape cookie cutters. Discard crusts.

**FOR WATERCRESS-BUTTER SANDWICHES:** In a bowl, stir together butter, lemon zest, chives, and salt. Spread one side of each bread slice with butter mixture. Divide watercress among 3 of the buttered bread slices. Top with remaining bread slices, butter side down. Cut each whole sandwich into 2 sandwiches with dinosaur-shapedcookie cutters. Discard crusts.

**FOR CURRIED EGG SALAD SANDWICHES:** In a bowl, stir together eggs, celery, red onion, cilantro, mustard, lime juice, mayonnaise, curry powder, and salt. Spread 3 bread slices with 1 tablespoon each of the mango chutney. Divide egg salad among the 3 bread slices spread with chutney. Top each with remaining bread slices. Cut each whole sandwich into 2 sandwiches with dinosaur-shape cookie cutters. Discard crusts.

**MAKE IT GLUTEN-FREE:** Use gluten-free bread.

**ALLERGENS:** Wheat, dairy

EASY   VEGETARIAN

# Chris' Salted Radish and Butter Bites

*"Did you know the key to a healthy urethra? Radishes!"* — Chris Traeger

Radishes may or may not contribute to high-functioning plumbing, but these herb-buttered baguette slices served with radishes and flaky salt for dipping are decidedly elegant. Inspired by a classic French hors d'oeuvre, the crisp, peppery radishes make a perfect foil for the rich herb butter. Leslie and Ben may even have sampled something similar on their getaway to Paris.

**SERVES 8 TO 10**
**PREP TIME:** 15 MINUTES

**WHAT YOU NEED**

⅓ cup butter, softened

2 tablespoons snipped fresh chives

1 (12-ounce) baguette

1 bunch radishes with tops, trimmed and
   root tips removed

¼ cup flaky sea salt, such as Maldon

**HOW YOU MAKE IT**

In a bowl, stir together butter and chives. Cut baguette in half crosswise, then cut halves lengthwise to make 8 to 10 bread sticks.

Spread butter on cut sides of bread sticks. Serve bread with radishes and salt for dipping.

**MAKE IT GLUTEN-FREE:** Use a gluten-free baguette.

**MAKE IT VEGAN:** Substitute a plant-based butter for the dairy butter.

**ALLERGENS:** Wheat, dairy

# Madame Secretary's Madeleines

You need a special pan to make these cakelike French cookies, but the end result—gorgeous scallop-shape cookies flavored with lemon and dipped in raspberry ganache—will make you feel as powerful as Leslie did wearing former Secretary of State Madeleine Albright's bald eagle pin on her lapel.

**MAKES 24 COOKIES**
**PREP TIME:** 1 HOUR
**COOK TIME:** 10 MINUTES

## WHAT YOU NEED

**FOR THE COOKIES**

2 large eggs, separated
½ cup sugar
½ cup butter, melted and cooled
½ teaspoon lemon zest
1 tablespoon fresh lemon juice
½ teaspoon pure vanilla extract
½ cup all-purpose flour
½ teaspoon baking powder
⅛ teaspoon baking soda
⅛ teaspoon kosher salt
¼ cup finely chopped pecans, toasted

**FOR THE RASPBERRY GANACHE**

⅓ cup heavy cream
4 ounces white baking chocolate
½ teaspoon raspberry extract
Pink gel or paste food coloring

## HOW YOU MAKE IT

**FOR THE COOKIES:** Preheat oven to 375°F. Butter and flour 24 madeleine molds.

In a bowl, combine egg yolks and sugar. Beat with an electric mixer on medium speed for 30 seconds. Add melted butter, lemon zest, lemon juice, and vanilla. Beat on low speed until combined.

In another bowl, stir together flour, baking powder, baking soda, and salt. Sprinkle flour mixture over egg yolk mixture; stir gently. Lightly beat egg whites. Stir egg whites and pecans into batter. Spoon batter into the prepared molds, filling each about half full.

Bake for 10 to 12 minutes or until the edges are golden and the tops spring back when lightly touched. Let stand for 1 minute in molds. Using the tip of a sharp knife, loosen cookies from the molds; invert onto a wire rack. Remove molds; cool completely on wire rack.

**FOR THE RASPBERRY GANACHE:** In a small saucepan, heat heavy cream over low heat just until boiling. Remove from heat. Immediately stir in baking chocolate until melted. Stir in extract. Tint pale pink with food coloring. Cool slightly.

Line a baking sheet with parchment paper. Using a soft brush, brush excess crumbs from cookies. Holding each cookie at an angle, dip narrow end halfway into ganache; let excess drip back into saucepan. Place on prepared baking sheet and let stand until ganache is set.

**MAKE IT GLUTEN-FREE:** Use a gluten-free flour blend in place of the all-purpose flour.

**ALLERGENS:** Wheat, dairy, soy

*EASY   VEGETARIAN*

# Thyme After Thyme Shortbread

*"You know this song already?"* — Ann Perkins

*"Of course I do. Everyone knows this song. It's amazing."* — April Ludgate

There's nothing like an epic Cyndi Lauper duet between frenemies to make a girl feel better—which both Ann and April did after raising the roof together in the conference room (with a little help from Donna). Fresh thyme—usually used in savory dishes—makes these sweet and buttery lemon-honey shortbreads sing in perfect harmony with a touch of earthy, minty herbiness.

**MAKES 36 COOKIES**
**PREP TIME**: 30 MINUTES
**COOK TIME**: 25 MINUTES

**WHAT YOU NEED**

1¾ cups all-purpose flour
½ cup powdered sugar
¼ cup yellow cornmeal
1 teaspoon chopped fresh thyme leaves
1 teaspoon lemon zest
2 tablespoons honey
¾ cup butter
Coarse sugar

**HOW YOU MAKE IT**

Preheat oven to 325°F. In a bowl, whisk together flour, powdered sugar, cornmeal, thyme, and lemon zest. Drizzle with honey (do not stir). Using a pastry blender, cut in butter until mixture resembles fine crumbs and starts to come together. Gently knead dough just until smooth; shape into a ball.

Line a cookie sheet with parchment paper. Pat dough into a 9-inch square. Using a fluted pastry wheel, cut into 36 squares. Do not separate. Sprinkle squares with coarse sugar. Bake for 25 to 30 minutes or until bottom starts to brown and center is set. Remove from the oven. Immediately recut the shortbread into squares with the pastry wheel.

Cool completely on cookie sheet on a wire rack.

**MAKE IT GLUTEN-FREE:** Use a gluten-free flour blend in place of the all-purpose flour.

**MAKE IT VEGAN:** Substitute plant-based butter for the dairy butter and pure maple syrup for the honey.

**ALLERGENS:** Wheat, dairy

# Powerful Women Flag Banner

*"I guess some people object to powerful depictions of awesome ladies."* — Leslie Knope

When Jerry paints *"The Centaur Goddess, Slaying a Great Stag"* for the Public Art Commission as a topless Leslie because, as he sheepishly admits, *"I've been thinking about powerful women, and subconsciously … I painted you,"* self-appointed morality monarch Marcia demands its destruction.

*"That painting is not gonna be destroyed. Every great work of art contains a message,"* Leslie retorts. *"And the message of this painting is, 'Get out of my way unless you want an arrow in your ass, Marcia.'"* The message of this work of art featuring your friends mixing it up with famous powerful women? Welcome to the club, ladies.

## WHAT YOU NEED

Banner pattern (page 143)
Pencil and tracing paper
Glue stick
Printer paper
8½-by-11-inch or 12-inch-square sheets of patriotic-print paper
⅜-inch-wide yellow check ribbon
16mm wood beads in red, blue, and yellow

## EQUIPMENT

Computer
Printer
Paper cutter (or scissors)
Paper punch

## HOW YOU MAKE IT

Search the internet for photos of powerful women who inspire you. Print the photos to fit the pendant pattern, enlarging or shrinking if needed. Also print friends' photos, if desired.

Trace the pendant pattern; cut out. Trace around the pattern on each photo; cut out.

Using a glue stick, attach the cutouts to printer paper; trim a ½-inch border. Attach the cutouts to patriotic papers. Trim each paper ¼ inch beyond the white paper.

Use a paper punch to make a hole at the top corners of the white border paper.

From the front, thread ribbon through a hole, across the back, and up through the second hole. Thread three wood beads on the ribbon. Continue connecting the flag shapes and adding the beaded patterns in this manner until complete. Once all pendants are connected, space them equally, as well as the beads.

# Heroines Photo Booth

If wearing Madeleine Albright's large, crystal-encrusted eagle lapel pin makes Leslie feel more powerful, think of how indomitable you and your friends will feel slipping on the iconic clothing and accessories of your heroines and snapping a pic for posterity.

## WHAT YOU NEED

Black fabric backdrop

Clothing and accessories, such as pantsuits, blouses with big collars or those that tie at the collar, skirts, high heels, big 1980s glasses, glittery brooches, goggles, scarves, etc. (second hand shops are good resources)

Life-size cutout of Leslie Knope's face (and/or other female heroines) attached to a large crafts stick

## HOW YOU MAKE IT

Find a space where you can attach the black fabric backdrop so it hangs flat, such as pinning it over a curtain rod, securing it on a railing, or using temporary hanging strips to attach it to a wall.

Organize props in containers such as baskets or boxes. Print two copies of each photo—one for your guest, and one to scrapbook.

# Rosie the Riveter Place Card Holders

*"Did you hear that? That was the sound of a glass ceiling being shattered."* — Leslie Knope

Or maybe that was Leslie knocking over a bunch of beer bottles in an attempt to infiltrate Pawnee City Hall's unofficial *"Boys' Club."* But her sentiment stands: As a woman, don't stay in your place in the public space. No superstar ever does!

## WHAT YOU NEED (FOR EACH HOLDER)

Wooden doll-shape peg

Marking pen

Artist paintbrushes

Acrylic paint in desired colors

Bandana and banner patterns (below)

Trims, including felt, fabric, and yarn

Two 3-inch-long pieces of chenille stem in desired flesh tone(s)

Red and white polka-dot fabric

Cardstock

## EQUIPMENT

Hand drill and small bit

Hot-glue gun and glue sticks

## HOW YOU MAKE IT

Secure the doll-shape peg with a clamp; drill ⅛-inch-deep holes on each side by shoulder area.

Draw simple clothing on the peg. Paint the clothing royal blue. Paint the face with appropriate flesh tone(s). Let dry. Draw or paint the face and hair; let dry.

Use the bandana pattern to cut out a tiny bandana. Tie the ends together and slip onto Rosie's head. Secure in place with hot glue if needed. Trim the figurine as desired using felt, fabric, and yarn.

For arms, hot-glue chenille stem ends into the drilled hole and shape like Rosie's famous pose. Be sure to leave a slot open for the place card.

Use the banner pattern to cut out each name tag. Handwrite a guest's name on a banner and slip it under Rosie's arm.

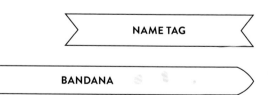

NAME TAG

BANDANA

# Ladies' Book Club

Let's face it: Book club is partly about expanding your mind, increasing your vocabulary, and engaging in stimulating conversation—but mostly it's about getting out of the house for the night with your lady friends for good food, wine, and camaraderie. Whether you're reading *The Time Traveler's Optometrist* or something a little more highbrow, book club never fails to rejuvenate.

EASY   GLUTEN-FREE   VEGAN

# Duke Silver's Incognito Mojito

*"A smooth and silky evening to you all. On nights like this, when the cold winds blow and the air is awash in the swirling eddies of our dreams, come with me and find safe haven ... in a warm bathtub full of my jazz."* — Duke Silver

Ron Swanson is a whiskey man, but surely mojitos are on the menu at Cozy's Bar, where his alter ego and the other members of The Duke Silver Trio play to an audience of middle-aged ladies who think he's "sex on a stick"—no doubt the topic of juicy conversation at some book clubs in Pawnee. This take on the classic Cuban cocktail features tequila instead of rum. Whether that will fool you into not recognizing it is anyone's guess—but does it really matter if it's as delicious as the original?

**SERVES 1**
**PREP TIME:** 10 MINUTES

**WHAT YOU NEED**

3 tablespoons fresh lime juice
4 teaspoons sugar
12 fresh mint leaves
Ice
¼ cup silver tequila
¼ cup club soda, chilled
Mint sprig and lime slice, for garnish

**HOW YOU MAKE IT**

In a highball or Collins glass, combine lime juice, sugar, and mint leaves. Mash mint leaves with the back of a spoon until the sugar dissolves. Fill glass with ice. Add tequila and club soda; stir to blend. Garnish with mint sprigs and lime slice.

**MAKE IT A MOCKTAIL:** Omit tequila. Use ½ cup club soda.

# April and Andy's Firecracker Shrimp

*"Give me the job! I'm April Ludgate, and my talent is explosive!"* — Andy Dwyer

Love inspires great deeds—and some really foolish ones, like wearing a mask of your beloved and throwing firecrackers at her potential employer to demonstrate her brilliance. Named for the explosive flavors of the sriracha-spiked sauce, this take on the classic Asian-inspired dish features baked shrimp instead of fried to avoid creating an Andy-level mess.

**SERVES 6 TO 8**
**PREP TIME**: 30 MINUTES
**COOK TIME**: 10 MINUTES

## WHAT YOU NEED

### FOR THE SHRIMP

3 tablespoons all-purpose flour
3 teaspoons five-spice powder
¼ teaspoon kosher salt
¼ teaspoon freshly ground black pepper
2 large eggs
2 cups panko bread crumbs
1 pound medium shrimp, peeled and deveined
Cooking spray

### FOR THE SAUCE

½ cup sweet chili sauce
¼ cup fresh orange juice
¼ cup soy sauce
2 tablespoons sriracha
3 cloves garlic, minced
2 teaspoons orange zest

## HOW YOU MAKE IT

**FOR THE SHRIMP**: Preheat oven to 400°F. Line a large rimmed baking pan with parchment paper. In a shallow bowl, whisk together flour, five-spice powder, salt, and pepper. In another shallow bowl, whisk eggs until well blended. Place bread crumbs in a third shallow bowl. Dip each shrimp in flour mixture, then eggs, then bread crumb mixture. Place on prepared pan. Mist with cooking spray. Bake for 10 to 12 minutes or until shrimp are pink and coating is golden brown, turning and misting with cooking spray halfway through baking.

**FOR THE SAUCE**: In a microwave-safe bowl, whisk together chili sauce, orange juice, soy sauce, sriracha, garlic, and orange zest.

Right before serving, microwave on high for 2 to 3 minutes or until heated through and slightly thickened. Transfer to a serving bowl. (To serve, have guests drizzle sauce over their shrimp.)

**MAKE IT GLUTEN-FREE**: Use gluten-free panko bread crumbs in place of the regular bread crumbs.

**ALLERGENS**: Wheat, soy, shellfish

EASY   GLUTEN-FREE

# 'Lament of the Buffalo' Wings

These may be named for one of the highly inappropriate murals in Pawnee's City Hall, but there's nothing unseemly about serving these vinegary, buttery, spicy, and saucy wings at book club. Just have lots of napkins on hand so no one smudges the pages of *The Time Traveler's Optometrist*—or whatever book you happen to be reading.

**SERVES 6 TO 8**
**PREP TIME**: 15 MINUTES
**COOK TIME**: 25 MINUTES

**WHAT YOU NEED**
16 chicken wings or drummettes (2 to 2¼ pounds)
Cooking spray
½ cup Buffalo-style hot sauce
⅓ cup butter, melted
Ranch or blue cheese dressing, for serving
Carrot and celery sticks, for serving

**HOW YOU MAKE IT**

Pat chicken dry with paper towels. Coat generously with cooking spray. Arrange half of the wings in an air fryer (avoid overcrowding). Cook at 400°F abouto 25 minutes or until skin is very crispy, turning halfway through cooking time. Repeat with remaining wings. (Keep cooked wings warm in a 200°F oven.)

Meanwhile, in a large bowl, whisk together hot sauce and butter. When all wings are cooked, add to the bowl and toss to coat. Serve immediately with dressing and carrot and celery sticks.

**OVEN METHOD:** Preheat oven to 500°F. Line a large rimmed baking pan with foil. Arrange all of the wings on the pan. Coat with cooking spray. Roast for 20 minutes, then turn wings. Roast an additional 10 minutes or until browned, crisp, and cooked through.

**ALLERGENS:** Dairy

# Garry's Mini Burritos with Guacamole Salsa

*"Damn, Jerry! You jumped into a creek for a burrito? What'd you do for a Klondike bar? Kill your wife?"*
— Leslie Knope, mimicking Tom Haverford

There are all kinds of love, and for lots of us—including Garry Gergich—food is one of them. And rest assured, these three-bite burritos are worth jumping into a creek for: Crisp-baked mini tortilla shells wrap around a cheesy rice-and-black-bean filling. A lemony-tart tomatillo-avocado salsa brings some chile heat.

**MAKES 24 BURRITOS**
**PREP TIME:** 45 MINUTES
**COOK TIME:** 25 MINUTES

## WHAT YOU NEED

### FOR THE GUACAMOLE SALSA

1 pound tomatillos, husked and rinsed
1 clove garlic, peeled
1 jalapeño chile, stemmed (seeded if desired)
1 serrano chile, stemmed (seeded if desired)
2 tablespoons chopped white onion
1 cup chopped fresh cilantro
1 large ripe avocado, halved and pitted
1 teaspoon kosher salt

### FOR THE BURRITOS

1 cup cooked long-grain rice
½ teaspoon kosher salt
2 teaspoons vegetable oil
2 tablespoons chopped fresh cilantro
2 teaspoons fresh lime juice
1 (15-ounce) can seasoned black beans
1½ cups finely shredded Monterey Jack cheese
6 (11-inch, extra-large burrito-style) flour tortillas, cut into quarters
Cooking spray

## HOW YOU MAKE IT

**FOR THE GUACAMOLE SALSA:** Combine tomatillos, garlic, jalapeño, and serrano in a pot. Cover with water. Bring to a boil. Reduce heat and simmer until tomatillos are very soft but have not begun to break apart, 10 to 12 minutes.

Using a slotted spoon, transfer tomatillos, chiles, and garlic to a blender. Add onion, cilantro, avocado flesh, and salt. Blend until smooth. (Salsa can be made 2 days ahead; cover surface with plastic wrap. Stir and bring to room temperature before serving.)

**FOR THE BURRITOS:** In a small microwave-safe bowl, warm the rice slightly, about 45 seconds. Fluff rice and stir in salt, vegetable oil, cilantro, lime juice, beans, and cheese.

Preheat oven to 425°F. Line a large rimmed baking pan with parchment paper. To assemble burritos, top each tortilla quarter with about 1 tablespoon of the rice mixture. Fold in the sides and roll up from the curved end of the tortilla toward the narrow end to create a mini burrito. Place, seam side down, on the prepared pan. Repeat with remaining tortillas and filling. Coat generously with cooking spray and bake about 15 minutes or until browned and crisp.

Serve with guacamole salsa for dipping.

**MAKE IT GLUTEN-FREE:** Use gluten-free tortillas in place of the flour tortillas.

**MAKE IT VEGAN:** Use plant-based cheese in place of the dairy cheese.

**ALLERGENS:** Wheat, dairy

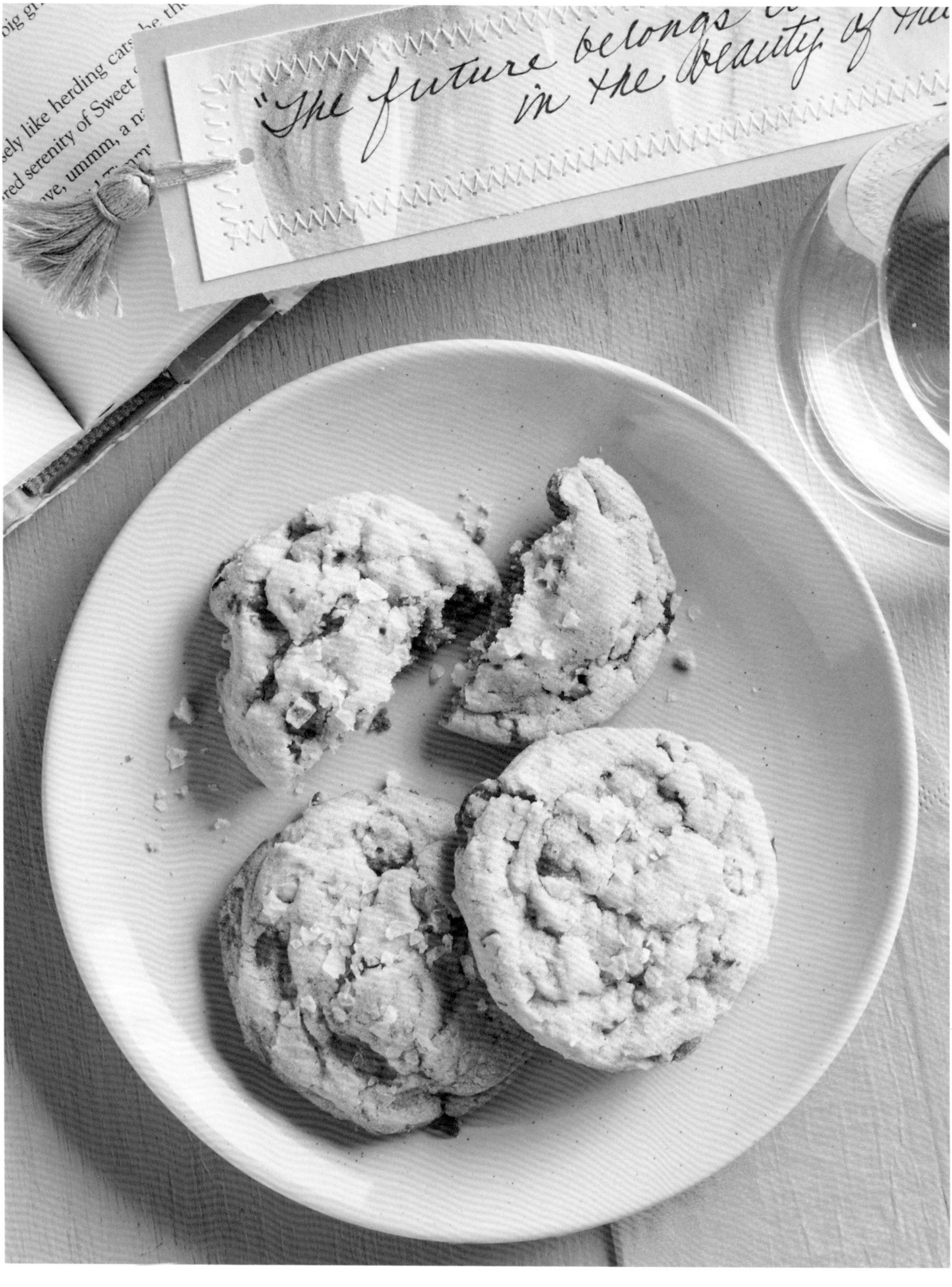
"The future belongs
in the beauty of

# Tom's Salty 'Hunk of Caramel' Cookies

*"I'll have another drink, and so will this adorable hunk of caramel to my right. Drink up, Tom. I'm going to powder my nose, amongst other things ... if you know what I mean."* — Joan Callamezzo

Given the beguiling combination of sweet and buttery caramel with flaky sea salt (and crunchy nuts, if you choose), guests will devour these cookies as hungrily as the rapacious host of *Pawnee Today* ravages the targets of her advances.

**MAKES ABOUT 36 COOKIES**
**PREP TIME**: 25 MINUTES
**COOK TIME**: 6 MINUTES

## WHAT YOU NEED

½ cup shortening
½ cup butter, softened
1 cup packed brown sugar
½ cup granulated sugar
1 teaspoon baking soda
2 large eggs
1 tablespoon pure vanilla extract
2¾ cups all-purpose flour
1 (11-ounce) package caramel bits (about 2 cups)
1½ cups chopped walnuts, pecans, or
  hazelnuts (optional)
Flaky sea salt, such as Maldon

## HOW YOU MAKE IT

Preheat oven to 375°F. Line 2 large cookie sheets with parchment paper.

In a large bowl, beat shortening and butter with an electric mixer on medium-high speed for 30 seconds. Add brown sugar, granulated sugar, and baking soda. Beat on medium speed 2 minutes, scraping bowl occasionally. Beat in eggs and vanilla until combined. Beat in as much of the flour as you can with the mixer. Using a wooden spoon, stir in any remaining flour. Stir in caramel bits and, if using, nuts.

Drop dough by heaping tablespoons 2 inches apart onto prepared pans. Sprinkle with flaky salt.

Bake for 6 to 8 minutes or until edges are lightly browned (cookies may not appear set). Cool on cookie sheets 2 minutes. Transfer cookies to a wire rack to cool.

**MAKE IT GLUTEN-FREE**: Use a gluten-free flour blend in place of the all-purpose flour.

**ALLERGENS**: Wheat, dairy, soy

# Female Authors Bingo

*"I wrote a book. The first historical guide to Pawnee. I wrote it as a reference for myself, but then my campaign adviser said we should make it a big wide release, so we had people contribute and we added pictures and removed a lot of my poems and emotional ramblings and pictures of unicorns, and here it is!"* — Leslie Knope

Leslie's book may not rank up there with *The Color Purple* or *Pride and Prejudice*, but it's definitely by a female author. Pick your favorite female authors to populate the cards of this sure-to-be-rousing bingo game.

## WHAT YOU NEED

Images and typed names of 10 to 24 favorite female authors (or handwritten names)

8½-by-11-inch pieces of cardstock

Image of author Leslie Knope for free space

1-inch wood discs (25 for each player)

Magazines or books to cut up

Glue stick

## EQUIPMENT

Computer

Printer

Circle cutter

## HOW YOU MAKE IT

To design the BINGO boards, write or type "Female Authors BINGO" at the top of the cardstock. Below that print a 7½-inch-square grid on cardstock, with five equal rows and five equal columns within the grid. This would make twenty-five 1½-inch squares.

Search the internet for photos of female authors who inspire you. Adjust/crop each photo to fit a 1⅝-inch square. Use a photo of Leslie Knope for the center FREE space.

If you're computer savvy and designing your BINGO cards in Word or a design program, copy the header and grid from step one and make multiple boards. Place the photos within the squares, adding the author's name below her photo, and making each card different. If creating the cards by hand, simply write the author's names in the squares on each card. Just remember to make each one different so all guests don't have BINGO at the same time. Print the boards.

To make the chips, use a ½-inch circle cutter to cut out type from magazines or old books. Use glue stick to adhere the circles to wood discs.

For the caller, print (or write out) the letters B, I, N, G, and O with each author's name on each card.

To play, the caller places the cards facedown, draws one at a time, then announces the drawn card. The players cover the author if they have her under the called letter. The game continues in this fashion until a player has covered all four corners or a horizontal, vertical, or diagonal line.

# Be Your Best Bookmarks

*"Leslie, could one say that a book is nothing more than a painting of words, which are the notes on the tapestry of the greatest film ever sculpted?"* — Derry Murbles, host of *Thoughts for Your Thoughts* on WYVS, Wamapoke County Public Radio

*"One could say that, but should one?"* — Leslie Knope

Don't lose your place in your current read the way Derry Murbles gets lost in his thoughts. These bookmarks featuring inspiring quotes from smart, powerful women will take you right where you left off, perfect for reading through one of Leslie's favorite books, her own *Pawnee: The Greatest Town in America.*

## WHAT YOU NEED
Waxed paper
Spray bottle filled with water
Heavyweight watercolor paper
Watercolor paints
Artists paintbrushes
Colored cardstock
White sewing thread
Black fine-point marking pen
Embroidery floss in desired color
Scissors

## EQUIPMENT
Paper cutter
Sewing machine
Hole punch

## HOW YOU MAKE IT
Cover work surface with waxed paper.

Mist a piece of watercolor paper with water. Keeping the colors light, paint the dampened watercolor paper, allowing the colors to naturally blend into one another. Let the paint dry.

Use a paper cutter to cut painted paper into 1½-by-7-inch strips.

For each bookmark, place a strip atop a piece of colored cardstock; use sewing machine to zigzag-stitch along each edge. Trim a narrow border.

Punch a hole centered in one end, approximately ½ inch from the edge.

Write a quote from your favorite heroine on each strip using a marking pen.

To make tassels, wrap embroidery floss around the tongs of a dinner fork 15 times. Thread a 10-inch-long piece of floss through the loops; knot tight. Remove from fork. Cut a 6-inch piece of floss; tie around tassel ¼ inch from top. Cut loops at opposite end. Knot long ends of floss at top of tassel. Thread the knot through the punched hole, then pull the tassel through the loop to secure it to the bookmark.

# Janet Snakehole's Undercover Book Cover

"*Joan Callamezzo started a book club four years ago, and now she is the literary tastemaker in the town: The Time Traveler's Optometrist, by Pawnee's own Penelope Foster, 'a heartwarming story about a caveman eye doctor who travels to present-day Cincinnati and can see everything but love.' Unreadable. Then, Joan slaps her sticker on it. Bestseller four years in a row.*" — Leslie Knope

The sparkly netted-veil disguise that helps turn April into her alter-ego, Janet Snakehole (the aristocratic widow with "a very terrible secret") may not fool anyone, but no one will know what you're reading when you wrap your book with this simple-to-make cover. (It also protects it from wear and tear.)

## WHAT YOU NEED

Heavy-duty art paper or wrapping paper,
  or wallpaper
Scissors

## HOW YOU MAKE IT

To get the proper-size cover, lay the book (opened) on the paper; fold over the first edge around the inside of the front cover so that it's 1 to 2 inches away from the binding. Then fold it around the back of the cover in the same way. There will be some extra paper, so make a mark an inch or so from the binding when the book is closed, and cut off the excess.

Fold the top and bottom to the size of the book. Line up the book with the bottom of the cover. Then fold up the top overlap. Continue the whole length of the cover, then fold it down.

Fold up the top overlap. Do that the whole length of the cover and then fold it down.

Slide the paper cover on so the book cover is inside the folds.

# Gal Pals'
# Cocktail Party

*"I could retire! But I wouldn't. I'm going to work until I'm 100. Then I'll cut back to four days a week."*
—Leslie Knope

While not everyone in the Pawnee Parks and Recreation Department works as hard as Leslie—and some may even actively avoid work—everyone needs to blow off some steam once in a while. Gather your best girls for an evening of nibbling and noshing, imbibing, and attempting to pin the tail on Li'l Sebastian.

# Joan Callamezzo's Gotcha! Martini

The *Pawnee Today* host is always shaking (and stirring!) things up with her explosive investigative journalism. Her take on this classic cocktail—gin, of course, minus the crushed aspirin rim—is delicious but powerful. Beware of its possible effects, which may include an inordinate lust for the spotlight.

**SERVES 1**
**PREP TIME:** 5 MINUTES

## WHAT YOU NEED
### FOR THE COCKTAIL
2½ ounces gin
½ ounce dry vermouth
Ice
Lemon peel twist or olives, for garnish

## EQUIPMENT
Cocktail shaker and/or large glass (depending on which method you choose)
Cocktail strainer (for stirred methodl)
Jigger or mini measuring glass
Martini or coupe glass

## HOW YOU MAKE IT

**SHAKE IT:** Place martini glass in the freezer to chill for 15 minutes. In a cocktail shaker, combine gin and dry vermouth. Add ice. Shake vigorously for 10 seconds. Strain martini into the chilled glass. To garnish with lemon peel, use a sharp paring knife to cut a strip of lemon peel from a lemon. Pinch the peel and rub it around the rim of the glass. Drop into the drink. Or garnish with an olive speared on a cocktail pick.

**STIR IT:** Place martini glass in the freezer to chill for 15 minutes. In a large glass, combine the gin and dry vermouth. Add ice and stir for 30 seconds or until martini is chilled. Strain martini into the chilled glass. Garnish as directed above.

# Chris' Positively Sparkling Ginger-Lemon-Honey Mocktail

*"I don't usually poison my body with dark alcohol, but this whiskey is EXCELLENT."* — Chris Traeger

If you—like Chris—look for healthier options to the status quo, shake up this bubbly beverage. It's just the thing to drink if your goal is to rise and shine before the sun and LITERALLY run to the moon.

**SERVES 1**

**PREP TIME:** 10 MINUTES

## WHAT YOU NEED

2 ounces bottled ginger juice

2 ounces fresh lemon juice

1 teaspoon honey

1 teaspoon warm water

Ice

Club soda, chilled

Lemon slice, for garnish

## EQUIPMENT

Cocktail shaker and/or large glass (depending on which method you choose)

Small glass

Cocktail strainer (for the stirred method)

Martini or coupe glass

## HOW YOU MAKE IT

**SHAKE IT:** Place martini glass in the freezer to chill for 15 minutes. In a cocktail shaker, combine ginger juice and lemon juice. In a small glass, stir together honey and warm water until honey dissolves. Add to shaker. Add ice. Shake vigorously for 10 seconds. Strain drink into the chilled martini glass. Top off with club soda. Garnish with lemon slice.

**STIR IT:** Place martini glass in the freezer to chill for 15 minutes. In a large glass, combine ginger juice and lemon juice. In a small glass stir together the honey and the warm water until honey dissolves. Add to large glass. Add ice and stir for 30 seconds or until drink is chilled. Strain drink into the chilled martini glass. Top off with club soda. Garnish with lemon slice.

# Donna's Sweet and Fiery Nut Mix

Until she settled in with Joe, Donna mixed it up with several paramours at a time in rotation. At once salty and sweet (a bit like Donna herself!), these smoky, crunchy nuts seasoned with a combination of warm and fiery spices just might get a man to commit arson for you.

---

**SERVES 12**
**PREP TIME**: 15 MINUTES
**COOK TIME**: 35 MINUTES

### WHAT YOU NEED

1 egg white

1 tablespoon water

1 pound raw whole cashews, whole almonds, walnut halves, and/or pecan halves (about 4 cups)

⅓ cup sugar

2 teaspoons kosher salt

1½ teaspoons ground cumin

1 teaspoon smoked paprika

1 teaspoon ground coriander

½ to ¾ teaspoon cayenne pepper

¼ teaspoon ground ginger

### HOW YOU MAKE IT

Preheat oven to 300°F. Line a large rimmed baking pan with parchment paper. In a bowl, beat egg white and the water until frothy. Add nuts and toss to coat. Place in a fine-mesh sieve set over a bowl to drain for 5 minutes.

In a large plastic bag, combine sugar, salt, cumin, smoked paprika, coriander, cayenne, and ginger. Add the nuts and shake well to coat. Spread nuts evenly in prepared pan.

Bake 35 to 40 minutes or until nuts are toasted and spice mixture is dry, stirring every 10 minutes. Remove from the oven and place nuts on a large sheet of foil to cool completely. When cool, break the nuts apart.

**ALLERGENS:** Nuts

# Wamapoke County Baked Brie

The people of Pawnee aren't renowned for much—perhaps most notably for their gluttonous ways. While they may most often feast on Big Belly Burgers from Paunch Burger and Meat Tornado Burritos from Big Head Joe's, special occasions call for something equally rich but far more elegant. This gooey baked Brie encased in flaky pastry features jam made from fruits the Wamapoke might have once gathered—a sweet complement to the richness of the buttery cheese. Serving it says "Wallaho mahk-a-tokeh," or "hello, honored guest." (Or, more accurately, "May you be blessed with a million possums.")

**SERVES 6 TO 8**

**PREP TIME**: 25 MINUTES

**COOK TIME**: 30 MINUTES

## WHAT YOU NEED

All-purpose flour, for dusting

1 sheet puff pastry, thawed according to package directions

1 (8-ounce) round Brie cheese

2 tablespoons tart cherry jam, plum jam, lingonberry preserves, or wild blueberry jam

¼ cup finely chopped pecans or walnuts, toasted

1 large egg

1 tablespoon water

Apple and/or pear slices

## HOW TO MAKE IT

Preheat oven to 400°F. Line a large rimmed baking pan with parchment paper; set aside.

Lightly dust a work surface with flour. Gently roll the thawed pastry sheet to an 11-inch square (don't press too hard or the pasty layers won't rise). Transfer to the prepared pan. Place Brie in the center of the pastry. Spread the jam on top of the cheese. Sprinkle with nuts.

Whisk together egg and the water. Bring one corner of the pastry up and over the Brie. Brush with egg wash. Continue to wrap the Brie, creating a pleated design, pressing down on the sides to remove air and brushing the pastry to help it stick. Gently press the edges and top to secure. Brush the tops and sides with egg wash.

Using a small sharp knife, make shallow scores on the surface about ½ inch apart and 1 inch long. (These allow steam to escape so the pastry doesn't get too puffy and separate from the cheese.)

Bake 30 to 35 minutes or until golden brown and crisp.

Cool in the pan for 5 to 10 minutes. Transfer to a serving platter and serve with apple and/or pear slices.

**MAKE IT GLUTEN-FREE**: Use gluten-free puff pastry dough in place of the regular puff pastry and a gluten-free flour blend in place of the all-purpose flour.

**ALLERGENS**: Wheat, dairy

# Ann's Beautiful Spinach-ster and Artichoke Dip

*"Oh, Ann, you beautiful spinster. I will find you love."* — Leslie Knope

You know you've got a keeper BFF when she works as hard as Leslie does to find Ann romance when she's *"in a bit of a lull."* Anyone lacking love will find it in this cheesy, rich, and gooey dip. Sure, it's been around awhile, but it never gets old.

---

**SERVES 8 TO 10**
**PREP TIME:** 20 MINUTES
**COOK TIME:** 30 MINUTES

### WHAT YOU NEED

1 (8-ounce) package cream cheese, softened
¾ cup mayonnaise
¾ cup sour cream
1 cup grated Parmesan cheese
1 cup shredded mozzarella cheese
½ cup shredded smoked Gouda cheese
1 (14-ounce) can artichoke hearts, drained and chopped
1 (10-ounce) package frozen spinach, thawed and squeezed dry
2 cloves garlic, minced
1 teaspoon lemon zest
½ teaspoon red pepper flakes (optional)
½ teaspoon kosher salt
¼ teaspoon freshly ground black pepper
Tortilla chips, toasted crostini, and raw vegetables, for serving

### HOW YOU MAKE IT

Preheat oven to 350°F. In a bowl, stir together cream cheese, mayonnaise, sour cream, ¾ cup of the Parmesan, ¾ cup of the mozzarella, the Gouda, artichoke hearts, spinach, garlic, lemon zest, red pepper flakes (if using), salt, and black pepper.

Transfer to a 1½- to 2-quart baking dish. Top with remaining ¼ cup each Parmesan and mozzarella. Bake for about 30 minutes or until bubbly and golden. (For a more golden-brown top, broil on high for 2 minutes.)

Serve hot with desired dippers.

**MAKE IT VEGAN:** Substitute plant-based cheeses for the dairy cheeses, plant-based sour cream for the dairy sour cream, and vegan mayonnaise for the regular mayonnaise.

**ALLERGENS:** Dairy

# Leslie's Cryptex Code Crackers

Ben may have been flummoxed by Leslie's cryptex that can be opened with *"the five-letter word that captures the essence of our third date,"* but there's no mystery to unravel when it comes to why these crackers are so good. Buttery, crispy, salty, tangy from buttermilk—with a little heat from a generous amount of black pepper—they're as satisfying to make as solving a puzzle.

**MAKES 24 CRACKERS**

**PREP TIME**: 30 MINUTES

**COOK TIME**: 15 MINUTES

## WHAT YOU NEED

1¾ cups all-purpose flour

¾ cup corn flour, such as Bob's Red Mill®

1 tablespoon sugar

½ teaspoon baking soda

¼ teaspoon kosher salt, plus more for sprinkling

2 tablespoons butter

1 cup buttermilk

¾ teaspoon coarse-ground black pepper, dried green peppercorns, or peppercorn blend

## HOW YOU MAKE IT

Preheat oven to 375°F. Line 2 large rimmed baking pans with parchment paper; set aside.

In a bowl, stir together all-purpose flour, corn flour, sugar, baking soda, and ¼ teaspoon salt. Use a pastry blender to cut in butter until mixture resembles coarse crumbs. Make a well in the center of the flour mixture. Add buttermilk. Using a fork, stir until mixture can be shaped into a ball.

Turn dough out onto a lightly floured surface. Knead for 8 to 10 strokes or until dough is almost smooth. Divide dough into 6 portions. Roll each into a 9-by-6-inch rectangle about ⅛ inch thick. Use a fluted pastry wheel or knife to cut each rectangle into quarters. Using a fork, prick rectangles all over. Place 1 inch apart on prepared pans.

Lightly brush crackers with water. Sprinkle with pepper and salt to taste. Bake about 15 minutes or until crisp. Remove from pan to wire racks to cool completely.

**MAKE IT GLUTEN-FREE**: Use a gluten-free flour blend in place of the all-purpose flour.

**MAKE IT VEGAN**: Use plant-based butter in place of the dairy butter. Use a double batch of vegan buttermilk (see page (page 33) in place of the dairy buttermilk.

**ALLERGENS**: Wheat, dairy

# Andy's Shrimp Claw Cocktail

*"There's so much free food at this party, honey. I love politics. Look, I made a shrimp claw."* — Andy Dwyer

Andy may have made his shrimp claw from breaded shrimp at a fancy political gala, but we would never suggest you do the same at a cocktail party with your besties. This lighter, more refined take on the shrimp claw calls for arranging chilled lemon-poached shrimp on martini glasses to resemble a delicate pink "claw" served with zesty cocktail sauce for dipping.

**SERVES 8**
**PREP TIME**: 30 MINUTES +1 HOUR CHILLING
**COOK TIME**: 5 MINUTES

## WHAT YOU NEED

**FOR THE SAUCE**

1 cup ketchup
3 tablespoons fresh lemon juice
2 tablespoons Worcestershire sauce
2 to 4 tablespoons prepared horseradish
1 clove garlic, minced
A few dashes hot sauce (optional)

**FOR THE SHRIMP**

2 large lemons
40 medium-large shrimp, shell left on
   (2 to 2¼ pounds)
Fresh dill sprigs

## HOW YOU MAKE IT

**FOR THE SAUCE**: In a bowl, stir together ketchup, lemon juice, Worcestershire sauce, horseradish, garlic, and hot sauce, if using. Cover and refrigerate at least 1 hour or overnight.

**FOR THE SHRIMP**: At least 2 hours before serving, fill a large pot with water. Cut 1 of the lemons in half. Squeeze the lemon juice into the water, then add lemon halves to the pot. Bring the water to boiling, then turn heat down so water is at a low simmer.

Add shrimp, cover the pot, and poach about 4 minutes. Check shrimp for doneness—they should be bright pink and firm. Remove pot from heat. Cover and let stand 2 minutes. Drain. When shrimp are cool enough to handle, shell and devein. Rinse under cool water and pat dry. Transfer to a bowl; cover and chill at least 2 hours.

To serve, cut remaining lemon into 8 wedges. Divide cocktail sauce among 8 chilled martini glasses (or other wide-mouthed glasses). Arrange 5 shrimp around one side of each glass, tail side out, to resemble a claw. Garnish each with a dill sprig.

**MAKE IT GLUTEN-FREE**: Use gluten-free Worcestershire sauce.

**ALLERGENS**: Shellfish

# Donna's Witty Wineglass Markers

*"I'm going to be direct and honest with you. I would like a glass of red wine, and I'll take the cheapest one you have, because I can't tell the difference."* — Leslie Knope

Whether your gal pals are Donna- or Craig-level wine connoisseurs or of the "just gimme what you got" persuasion, everyone will be able to tell the difference between their glass of wine and someone else's with these whimsical wine charms ringing the stems.

## WHAT YOU NEED

Waxed paper

Oven-bake clay in golden brown, white, and red

Pencil with an unused eraser

Small paring knife

Skewer, awl, toothpick, or similar item

3-inch piece of ball chain with clasp

## EQUIPMENT

Oven

## HOW YOU MAKE IT

Cover the work surface with waxed paper.

To make the waffle, roll a ball of golden brown clay approximately the size of a large grape; press flat with palm of your hand.

To make a tool for impressing the waffle pattern into the clay, cut off the rounded edges of the pencil eraser using a paring knife. This will leave a small square of eraser in the center. Starting near the center of the clay, press the eraser into the clay and remove it. Make a row of squares across the clay, leaving a little clay between each imprint. Continue working in this manner until the entire piece is imprinted.

For the whipped cream, roll a tiny snake from white clay. Shape the piece into a small coil until the desired size is achieved. Break off any excess. Gently press onto the waffle.

For strawberries, roll tiny egg shapes from red clay. Use a skewer or similar item to make seed indentations in the clay. Decide on placement and press strawberries gently into clay.

Using the skewer or similar tool, make a small hole near the edge of the waffle. Make it big enough for the chain to slip through.

To make the coffee-filled mug, roll a tube from golden brown clay approximately the diameter of a jellybean. Use a knife to cut off a ½-inch-long piece.

Use a rolling pin to flatten a piece of white clay to approximately $\frac{1}{16}$ inch thick.Use a knife to cut a ⅝-inch-wide strip from clay. Cut one end straight. Aligning one edge of the brown clay with one edge of the white clay, roll the white clay around the brown; cut off excess white clay.

To make the mug bottom, place the mug onto flattened white clay. Cut around the mug shape; gently smooth onto bottom of mug.

Shape a small handle from white clay; gently press onto mug.

For lettering roll a very tiny snake from red clay. Shape into two Js, an apostrophe, and an S. Gently press onto mug.

Bake the shapes in the oven according to the clay manufacturer's directions. Let cool completely before handling.

To attach the charms to a wineglass stem, insert ball chain through the hole in the waffle or the handle in the mug. Wrap the ball chain around the stem; secure the clasp.

# Rosie the Riveter We Can Do It! Bandana Cocktail Napkins

For the Pawnee City Manager's Office Halloween screening of *Death Canoe 4: Murder at Blood Lake*, Leslie dons coveralls and a red bandana to rep one of her greatest heroine role models. Every dab of the lips with these napkins delivers a dose of female empowerment.

**WHAT YOU NEED (FOR EACH NAPKIN)**

Scissors

11-inch square red-and-white polka-dot fabric

White embroidery floss

Embroidery needle

½-inch red-and-white polka-dot button

¾-inch white button

**EQUIPMENT**

Iron

**HOW YOU MAKE IT**

Fold each edge of fabric square under ¼ inch; press. Fold under ¼ inch again; press.

Using white embroidery floss, secure the hemmed edges with blanket stitches.

Stack polka-dot button on white button; sew to one corner of the napkin. Knot the floss ends on top of the button; trim ends short.

# Pin the Tail on Li'l Sebastian

*"Li'l Sebastian, we miss you. But we know you are in heaven, looking down on us, doing your two favorite things: eating carrots and urinating freely. So gallop on, Li'l Sebastian, in that big horsey ring in the sky."* — Leslie Knope

Celebrate Li'l Sebastian—Pawnee's favorite miniature horse (not a pony!)—by having a cocktail or two with friends—then play a party game that involves a blindfold and safety pins! (Be careful, safety pins are sharp.)

## WHAT YOU NEED

Patterns (page 143)
Printer paper
Tape (optional)
Faux fur in brown
Black marking pen
Scissors
20-by-30-inch piece of foam board
Hot-glue gun and glue sticks
Off-white yarn
Extra-large safety pins
½-inch ribbon in a different color for each guest
Blindfold, such as a bandana

## EQUIPMENT

Copier

## HOW YOU MAKE IT

Copy the patterns, enlarging as indicated and taping together if needed.

Place patterns on the back of the faux fur so that Li'l Sebastian's head is facing right. Trace around the patterns using a black marking pen. Cut out the shapes.

Attach Li'l Sebastian's body, fur side up, to the foam board using hot glue. Attach the ears where indicated.

Hot-glue strands of off-white yarn along the top edge of Li'l Sebastian's head and mane area. Using the photo as a guide, trim the yarn to lengths that mimic Li'l Sebastian's.

For each tail, cut eight 12-inch-long pieces of yarn. These will be folded over to make a 6-inch tail. Working one strand at a time, fold yarn in half. Thread the loop of the yarn through a safety pin. Secure it to the nonopening side of the safety pin by threading the yarn ends through the loop; pull snug. Repeat for each piece of yarn. Tie a ribbon bow around the yarn near the safety pin. Use a different color yarn for each tail so they can be identified.

Give each guest a tail. Before their turn, open the safety pin and blindfold the player.

Spin the player around once or twice and face them toward the board. Using one hand only, let the player poke the tail into Li'l Sebastian.

# Besties' Date Night In

"One time, I accidentally drank an entire bottle of vinegar—I thought it was terrible wine. Once I went out with a guy who wore 3D glasses the entire evening. One time, I rode in a sidecar on a guy's motorcycle and the sidecar detached and went down a flight of stairs. Another time, I went to a really boring movie with a guy and while I was asleep, he tried to pull out one of my teeth. I literally woke up with his hand in my mouth. We went out a couple times after that, but then he got weird."
—Leslie Knope

Want to avoid a date as awful as Leslie's terrible experiences? Make one with your BFF. You're guaranteed a good time spending an evening sharing a special meal with one of your most important people.

# 'You Like Potato and I Like Potahto' Soup

Mouse Rat rocked the house at the "Oldies But Goodies!" Valentine's Day dance at the Pawnee Senior Center. Cake and punch were served, and there was much shuffling on the dance floor. Despite Andy's initial reservations that he "sucked" as a crooner after rehearsing "You Like Potato and I Like Potahto" before the dance, by the end of the evening—after a flirtation with an admiring octogenarian—he figured he'd "nailed the gig." Serve this universally loved rich and creamy soup as a starter, and you'll nail the gig, too—no matter who you're hosting.

**SERVES 2**
**PREP TIME:** 30 MINUTES
**COOK TIME:** 30 MINUTES

## WHAT YOU NEED

**FOR THE CROUTONS**
2 slices firm white bread
4 tablespoons butter

**FOR THE SOUP**
2 tablespoons butter
2 leeks, roughly chopped (white and light green parts only)*
1 clove garlic, smashed and peeled
1 pound Yukon gold potatoes, peeled and chopped
3½ cups chicken broth
1 bay leaf
1 sprig fresh thyme
½ teaspoon kosher salt
⅛ teaspoon freshly ground black pepper
½ cup heavy cream
1 tablespoon finely chopped fresh chives

## HOW YOU MAKE IT

**FOR THE CROUTONS:** Cut two 2½-inch heart shapes from each slice of bread with a heart-shape cookie cutter. In a medium nonstick skillet, melt the butter over low heat. Increase heat to medium and add bread cutouts. Cook for 2 to 2½ minutes or until toasts are golden brown on one side. Lower the heat slightly. Turn and cook for 1 to 1½ minutes on the other side, until golden brown on both sides. Place on a paper towel-lined plate; set aside.

**FOR THE SOUP:** In a medium pot, melt butter over medium heat. Add leeks and garlic and cook, stirring frequently, for 10 minutes or until soft and wilted (do not brown).

Add potatoes, broth, bay leaf, thyme, salt, and pepper to the pot. Bring to a boil. Turn heat to low and simmer, covered, for 15 minutes or until potatoes are very soft.

Remove bay leaf and thyme sprig. Purée soup with a hand held immersion blender until very smooth. (Or use a regular blender, being careful to allow steam to escape.) Add cream and bring to a simmer. Taste and adjust seasoning, if necessary. Stir in chives.

Divide soup between 2 warmed soup bowls. Top each with two heart-shape croutons.

*****NOTE:** Leeks can have sand grit in between their layers. To clean, cut in half lengthwise and fan the layers under cool running water before chopping. Alternatively, cut in half lengthwise and slice, then swish in cool water in a salad spinner. Spin dry.

**MAKE IT GLUTEN-FREE:** Use gluten-free bread to make the croutons.

**MAKE IT VEGAN:** Use plant-based butter in place of the dairy butter and plant-based heavy cream in place of the dairy heavy cream. Use vegetable broth in place of the chicken broth.

**MAKE IT VEGETARIAN:** Use vegetable broth in place of the chicken broth.

**ALLERGENS:** Wheat, dairy

# Bibb Lettuce Salad with Green (Pawnee) Goddess Dressing

*"I am a goddess, a glorious female warrior, queen of all that I survey. Enemies of fairness and equality, hear my womanly roar! Yeeahhhh!"*
— Pawnee Goddess Oath

This salad is plated in the manner befitting a Pawnee Goddess. Each buttery head of lettuce is disassembled, dressed in a brightly flavored lemony herb vinaigrette, then reassembled on the plate and sprinkled with more fresh herbs for a perfect presentation. It's trophy-worthy!

**SERVES 2**
**PREP TIME:** 30 MINUTES

### WHAT YOU NEED

¼ cup Champagne vinegar or white wine vinegar

¼ cup fresh lemon juice

¼ cup each coarsely chopped fresh basil, chives, parsley, and tarragon

1 small shallot, minced

2 tablespoons honey

1 cup extra-virgin olive oil

1 teaspoon kosher salt

Freshly ground black pepper

2 small heads Bibb lettuce

Minced fresh chives and whole small fresh basil, parsley, and tarragon leaves, for garnish

### HOW YOU MAKE IT

In a blender or food processor, combine vinegar, lemon juice, herbs, shallot, and honey. Blend until mixture is finely chopped. With the blender running, slowly drizzle in the olive oil until smooth. Transfer to a jar with a lid.

Stir in salt and pepper, adjusting seasoning to taste if necessary. Refrigerate until ready to use (up to 1 week).

To build the salads, work with one head of lettuce at a time. Separate the leaves. Wash in cold water, then spin dry in a salad spinner; set aside. Repeat with the other head of lettuce.

Place the leaves from 1 head of lettuce in a bowl. Drizzle with 1 tablespoon vinaigrette. On a chilled salad plate, arrange the outer lettuce leaves as a base, then rebuild each head of lettuce, ending with the smallest leaves. Repeat with the other head of lettuce.

Drizzle each salad with a little additional vinaigrette. Sprinkle with minced chives and basil, parsley, and tarragon leaves. Serve immediately.

# Ron's Whiskey-Glazed Steak

*"After I've had too much whiskey, I cook myself a large flank steak pan-fried in salted butter. I eat that, put on a pair of wet socks, and go to sleep."* — Ron Swanson

Two of Ron's favorite things come together in this sweet and savory glazed steak. Marinate the steak overnight for optimum flavor and efficiency when making your date-night menu.

---

**SERVES 2**

**PREP TIME**: 10 MINUTES + 4 HOURS MARINATING

**COOK TIME**: 8 MINUTES

### WHAT YOU NEED

2 tablespoons Worcestershire sauce

2 tablespoons tamari or soy sauce

1 tablespoon balsamic vinegar

3 tablespoons pure maple syrup

¼ cup + 1 tablespoon whiskey or bourbon

1 clove garlic, minced

Freshly ground black pepper

1 (12- to 14-ounce) New York strip steak, about 1 inch thick

1 tablespoon butter

Kosher salt (optional)

### HOW YOU MAKE IT

In a small bowl, whisk together Worcestershire, tamari, balsamic vinegar, 2 tablespoons of the maple syrup, the ¼ cup whiskey, the garlic, and pepper to taste.

Place steak in a resealable plastic bag and pour the marinade over. Seal bag, turning to coat steak. Place on a plate and marinate in the refrigerator for at least 4 hours or overnight, turning occasionally.

Remove steak from the refrigerator 30 minutes before cooking. Melt butter in a heavy skillet over high heat. Remove the steak from marinade, letting excess marinade drip off. Place steak in the hot skillet. Cook for 3 minutes or until browned on one side. Turn and cook for 3 minutes more, or until browned on both sides.

Stir together the remaining 1 tablespoon maple syrup and whiskey in a small bowl. Pour over steak and continue cooking, spooning glaze over steak, for 1½ to 2 minutes or until steak has caramelized and turned a rich brown color.

Remove steak from pan. Cover loosely with foil and let stand 10 minutes. To serve, season with additional pepper and salt, if desired. Slice against the grain.

**MAKE IT GLUTEN-FREE:** Use gluten-free Worcestershire sauce and gluten-free tamari or soy sauce.

**ALLERGENS:** Dairy, wheat, soy

# April's Black Coffee Martini with 'Extra Grounds'

This cocktail is a bit like April—it may look dark, brooding, and bitter from the outside, but once you get to know it better, you discover it's actually quite sweet.

**SERVES 1**
**PREP TIME:** 10 MINUTES

**WHAT YOU NEED**

2 chocolate wafer cookies
Chocolate syrup
Ice
2 ounces vodka
½ ounce coffee liqueur, such as Kahlúa
1 ounce cold brew concentrate
½ ounce simple syrup

**HOW YOU MAKE IT**

Place cookies in a plastic bag. Roll over cookies with a rolling pan or heavy can to finely crush. Pour crumbs onto a plate. On another plate, draw a circle the size of your martini glass rim in chocolate syrup. Invert glass and dip the rim in syrup, then immediately in chocolate cookie crumbs. Turn upright. Place in freezer for 15 minutes.

Fill a cocktail shaker with ice. Add vodka, coffee liqueur, cold brew concentrate, and simple syrup to shaker. Shake vigorously for 30 seconds. Strain into chilled martini glass.

**MAKE IT GLUTEN-FREE:** Use gluten-free chocolate wafer cookies in place of the regular chocolate wafer cookies.

**ALLERGENS:** Wheat, soy

# Roses Are Red Centerpiece

This simple centerpiece sends a heartfelt message: Roses are red, violets are blue, you're my bestie, and I love you.

**WHAT YOU NEED**

Wet-style florists foam
Knife
Heart-shape dish
Water
Garden snippers
Red roses
Scissors
Narrow silver ribbon
Quilting pin
Faux berries

**HOW YOU MAKE IT**

Using a knife, cut the florists foam to fill the heart-shape dish. Wedge foam into dish; saturate with water.

Cut rose stems to 4 inches.

Poke the rose stems into the foam in an evenly spaced manner, covering the foam

Tie a bow using several strands of narrow silver ribbon; attach it using a quilting pin. Add to the focal point by adding faux berries and rose leaves.

# Friendship Charm Bracelets

Leslie Knope approaches gift-giving like it's a fierce competition, "finding or making that perfect something," she says. "It's also like a sport to me because I always win."

Whether it's Breakfast Day, Friends Week, or Galentine's Day, you'll win the gift exchange with these charming bracelets celebrating your BFF's likes, loves, and life.

## WHAT YOU NEED
Charms relating to party guests
Solid or link charm bracelet
Beads or bead charms for spacers

## HOW YOU MAKE IT
Attach charms to the desired style of charm bracelet. Add spacers, if desired, to fill.

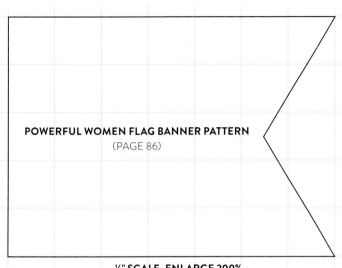

**POWERFUL WOMEN FLAG BANNER PATTERN**
(PAGE 86)

½" SCALE, ENLARGE 200%

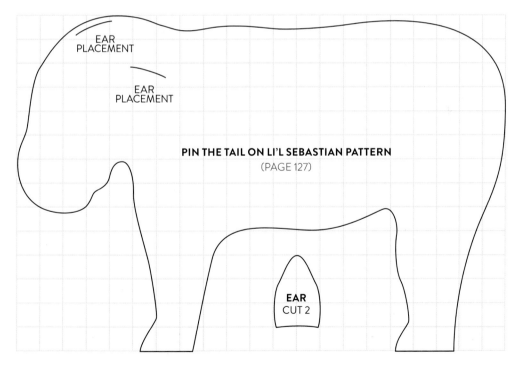

**PIN THE TAIL ON LI'L SEBASTIAN PATTERN**
(PAGE 127)

EAR
PLACEMENT

EAR
PLACEMENT

**EAR**
CUT 2

¼" SCALE, ENLARGE 400%

# TITAN
# BOOKS

144 Southwark Street
London SE1 0UP
www.titanbooks.com

Find us on Facebook: www.facebook.com/TitanBooks
Follow us on Twitter: @TitanBooks

**peacock**

Published by Titan Books, London, in 2022.

A CIP catalogue record for this title is available from the British Library.

ISBN: 978-1-80336-332-5

INSIGHT EDITIONS
Publisher: Raoul Goff
VP of Licensing and Partnerships: Vanessa Lopez
VP of Creative: Chrissy Kwasnik
VP of Manufacturing: Alix Nicholaeff
VP, Editorial Director: Vicki Jaeger
Editors: Justin Eisinger and Harrison Tunggal
Managing Editor: Maria Spano
Production Associate: Deena Hashem
Senior Production Manager, Subsidiary Rights: Lina s Palma-Temena

WATERBURY PUBLICATIONS, INC.
Editorial Director: Lisa Kingsley
Creative Director: Ken Carlson
Associate Editor: Maggie Glisan
Associate Editor: Tricia Bergman
Associate Art Director: Doug Samuelson
Photographer: Ken Carlson
Food Stylist: Jennifer Peterson
Food Stylist Assistant: Holly Wiederin

Insight Editions, in association with Roots of Peace, will plant two trees for each tree used in the manufacturing of this book. Roots of Peace is an internationally renowned humanitarian organization dedicated to eradicating land mines worldwide and converting war-torn lands into productive farms and wildlife habitats. Roots of Peace will plant two million fruit and nut trees in Afghanistan and provide farmers there with the skills and support necessary for sustainable land use.

Manufactured in China by Insight Editions

10 9 8 7 6 5 4 3 2 1